Unlocking AI: A Simple Guide for Beginners

Rajamanickam Antonimuthu

Rajamanickam.Com

For many years, I have been uploading numerous news videos about Artificial Intelligence (AI) innovations and organizing them into a playlist. Whenever I go through that playlist, I wonder at the amazing and rapid growth of AI. Though there is a lot of hype surrounding AI, many people are still unaware of its power, especially when it comes to how AI can truly help them in their daily lives and at workplaces. So, I decided to write this book to help people learn about AI. I have already published many books discussing advanced AI topics (e.g., RAG), but this book is for beginners who are eager to explore the power of AI. I have released AI Course also.

1. Introduction: What is AI and Why Should You Care?

Artificial Intelligence, or AI, is a fascinating field that's all about teaching machines to think and act like humans—or even smarter than humans in some cases. But don't worry, it's not as complicated as it sounds! Let's break it down.

What is AI?

At its core, AI is about creating computer systems that can perform tasks that usually require human intelligence. These tasks include things like:

- Recognizing faces in photos.
- Understanding spoken language (like when you talk to Siri or Alexa).
- Recommending movies or songs you might like (Netflix and Spotify!).
- Even driving cars autonomously (self-driving cars).

AI systems learn from data and experiences, just like humans do. For example, if you show an AI system thousands of pictures of cats, it can learn to recognize a cat in a new picture it's never seen before. This ability to learn and improve over time is what makes AI so powerful.

AI is Everywhere

You might not realize it, but AI is already a big part of your daily life. Here are some examples:

- **Smartphones:** AI powers features like facial recognition, predictive text, and voice assistants.
- **Social Media:** AI decides what posts you see on your feed and helps detect fake news or harmful content.
- **Online Shopping:** AI recommends products you might like based on your browsing history.
- **Navigation Apps:** AI helps you find the fastest route to your destination by analyzing traffic patterns.

How Does AI Work?

AI works by using algorithms, which are like step-by-step instructions for solving a problem. These algorithms process large amounts of data to find patterns and make decisions. For example:

- If you're using a spam filter in your email, AI analyzes the content of emails to decide which ones are spam.
- If you're using a fitness app, AI might analyze your workout data to suggest personalized exercise plans.

The more data an AI system has, the better it gets at its job. This is why companies collect so much data—it helps them build smarter AI systems.

AI is Not Magic

While AI can seem like magic, it's really just a combination of math, data, and clever programming. It's not about creating robots that can take over the world (despite what movies might show!). Instead, AI is about building tools that can make our lives easier, safer, and more efficient.

Why Should You Care About AI?

AI is transforming the world around us, and understanding it can help you:

- Stay informed about the technology shaping our future.
- Make better decisions about the tools and apps you use.
- Explore exciting career opportunities in a fast-growing field.

In short, AI is not just for scientists or tech experts—it's for everyone. And the best part? You don't need to be a genius to understand it. By the end of this book, you'll have a solid grasp of what AI is, how it works, and why it matters.

2. A Brief History of AI: From Myths to Reality.

Artificial Intelligence might seem like a modern invention, but its roots go back centuries. From ancient myths to groundbreaking scientific discoveries, the story of AI is as rich and exciting as the technology itself. Let's take a trip through time to see how AI evolved into what it is today.

Ancient Myths and Early Dreams of AI

Long before computers existed, humans dreamed of creating intelligent machines. These ideas often appeared in myths and stories:

- **Greek Mythology:** Tales of mechanical servants, like the bronze giant Talos, who guarded the island of Crete.
- **Ancient China:** Stories of artificial beings, such as the mechanical engineer Yan Shi, who reportedly created a lifelike humanoid robot.
- **Medieval Legends:** Alchemists and inventors imagined creating artificial life, like the Golem of Jewish folklore, a clay creature brought to life through magic.

These stories show that the desire to create intelligent machines has been part of human imagination for thousands of years.

The Birth of Modern AI: The 20th Century

The real journey of AI began in the 20th century, when scientists started turning these dreams into reality. Here are some key milestones:

- **1950: Alan Turing and the Turing Test**
  British mathematician Alan Turing proposed the idea of a machine that could think. He introduced the *Turing Test*, a way to determine if a machine could exhibit intelligent behavior indistinguishable from a human.
- **1956: The Dartmouth Conference**
  This is considered the official birth of AI as a field. Scientists like John McCarthy, Marvin Minsky, and others gathered at Dartmouth College to discuss how machines could simulate human intelligence. The term "Artificial Intelligence" was coined here.
- **1960s: Early Optimism and the First AI Programs**
  Early AI programs like the *Logic Theorist* and *ELIZA* (a chatbot that simulated conversation) showed promise. People were optimistic that machines would soon match human intelligence.

The AI Winters: Setbacks and Challenges

Despite early excitement, progress in AI faced significant challenges:

- **1970s-1980s: The First AI Winter**
  Funding and interest in AI declined as early systems failed to deliver on their promises. Computers weren't powerful enough, and data was scarce.
- **1990s: The Second AI Winter**
  AI faced another slowdown as researchers struggled to overcome technical limitations.

However, this period also saw the rise of practical applications, like expert systems used in medicine and business.

The AI Renaissance: The 21st Century Boom

The 21st century brought a resurgence of interest in AI, thanks to three key factors:

1. **More Data:** The internet and digital devices generated vast amounts of data, which AI systems could use to learn.
2. **Better Algorithms:** Advances in machine learning, especially deep learning, allowed AI to solve complex problems.
3. **Faster Computers:** Powerful processors and GPUs made it possible to train AI models quickly.

Some landmark achievements include:

- **1997:** IBM's Deep Blue defeated world chess champion Garry Kasparov.
- **2011:** IBM's Watson won the game show *Jeopardy!*, showcasing its ability to understand natural language.
- **2016:** Google's AlphaGo defeated the world champion in Go, a game far more complex than chess.
- **2020s:** Generative AI tools like ChatGPT and DALL·E revolutionized how we interact with machines, creating text, images, and even music.

AI Today: A Transformative Force

Today, AI is everywhere—from voice assistants and self-driving cars to medical diagnostics and creative tools. It's no longer just a scientific curiosity; it's a technology that's reshaping industries and changing the way we live.

What's Next for AI?

The history of AI is still being written. As we look to the future, questions about ethics, regulation, and the potential for superintelligent machines remain. But one thing is certain: AI will continue to evolve, and its impact on our world will only grow.

3. How Does AI Work? Demystifying the Basics

Artificial Intelligence might seem like a mysterious black box, but at its core, it's built on a few key ideas that are easy to understand once you break them down. In this chapter, we'll explore how AI works, from the basics of machine learning to the role of data and algorithms. Let's dive in!

What is Machine Learning?

Machine Learning (ML) is the backbone of most modern AI systems. It's a way for computers to learn from data without being explicitly programmed. Here's how it works:

- **Step 1: Data Collection**
  AI systems need data to learn. This could be anything from pictures of cats to customer purchase histories.
- **Step 2: Training the Model**
  The data is fed into an algorithm, which looks for patterns and learns to make predictions or decisions.
- **Step 3: Testing and Improving**
  The model is tested on new data to see how well it performs. If it makes mistakes, it's adjusted and trained again.

For example, if you want an AI system to recognize dogs in photos, you'd show it thousands of pictures of dogs (and non-dogs) so it can learn the difference.

Types of Machine Learning

There are three main types of machine learning, each with its own approach:

1. **Supervised Learning**
   - The AI is given labeled data (e.g., pictures of cats labeled "cat" and pictures of dogs labeled "dog").
   - It learns to map inputs to the correct outputs.
   - Example: Spam filters that learn to classify emails as "spam" or "not spam."
2. **Unsupervised Learning**
   - The AI is given unlabeled data and must find patterns on its own.
   - Example: Grouping customers into segments based on their shopping behavior.
3. **Reinforcement Learning**
   - The AI learns by trial and error, receiving rewards for good actions and penalties for bad ones.
   - Example: Training a robot to walk or a computer program to play a game.

Neural Networks and Deep Learning

Neural networks are a type of machine learning inspired by the human brain. They consist of layers of interconnected nodes (or "neurons") that process data. Here's how they work:

- **Input Layer:** Receives the data (e.g., pixels from an image).
- **Hidden Layers:** Process the data, extracting features and patterns.
- **Output Layer:** Produces the final result (e.g., "cat" or "dog").

When neural networks have many layers, they're called *deep learning* models. These are especially good at handling complex tasks like image and speech recognition.

The Role of Algorithms

Algorithms are the step-by-step instructions that tell AI systems how to process data and make decisions. Some common AI algorithms include:

- **Decision Trees:** Used for classification and regression tasks.
- **Support Vector Machines (SVM):** Great for finding patterns in data.

- **K-Means Clustering:** Used in unsupervised learning to group similar data points.

The Importance of Data

Data is the fuel that powers AI. Without data, AI systems can't learn or improve. Here's why data matters:

- **Quantity:** More data usually means better performance, as the AI has more examples to learn from.
- **Quality:** Clean, accurate data is essential. Garbage in, garbage out!
- **Diversity:** Diverse data helps prevent bias and ensures the AI works well for everyone.

Putting It All Together: How AI Makes Decisions

Let's say you're using a music streaming app that recommends songs. Here's how AI might work behind the scenes:

1. The app collects data about your listening habits (e.g., genres, artists, playlists).
2. A machine learning model analyzes this data to find patterns (e.g., you love jazz on rainy days).
3. The model predicts what songs you might like and recommends them.

This process happens in seconds, thanks to the power of AI!

AI Isn't Perfect

While AI is incredibly powerful, it's not flawless. It can make mistakes, especially if the data is biased or incomplete. That's why human oversight is still important.

Why Does This Matter to You?

Understanding how AI works helps you:

- Make informed decisions about the technology you use.
- Spot potential issues, like bias or privacy concerns.
- Appreciate the incredible science behind the tools that make your life easier.

4. Types of AI: Narrow AI, General AI, and Superintelligence

When people talk about Artificial Intelligence, they're often referring to different types of AI systems. These range from the practical tools we use every day to the futuristic visions of machines that surpass human intelligence. In this chapter, we'll explore the three main categories of AI: Narrow AI, General AI, and Superintelligence.

1. Narrow AI (Weak AI): The AI We Use Today

Narrow AI is designed to perform specific tasks. It's the most common form of AI and the one you interact with daily. Here's what makes Narrow AI special:

- **Task-Specific:** It excels at one thing but can't do anything outside its programmed scope.
- **Examples in Action:**
  - **Voice Assistants:** Siri, Alexa, and Google Assistant can answer questions and control smart devices but can't write a novel or drive a car.
  - **Recommendation Systems:** Netflix suggests movies, and Amazon recommends products based on your preferences.
  - **Image Recognition:** Apps like Google Photos can identify objects, people, and even pets in your pictures.
- **Limitations:** Narrow AI doesn't understand context or have consciousness. It's just following patterns in data.

---

2. General AI (Strong AI): The Dream of Human-Like Intelligence

General AI, also known as Strong AI or Artificial General Intelligence (AGI), refers to machines that can think and reason like humans. Unlike Narrow AI, General AI would be capable of:

- **Learning Any Task:** It could perform any intellectual task that a human can do, from solving complex problems to creating art.
- **Understanding Context:** It would have common sense and the ability to apply knowledge across different situations.
- **Self-Awareness:** Some visions of General AI include machines that are conscious and aware of their existence.

Why Don't We Have General AI Yet?

Creating General AI is incredibly challenging because it requires:

- A deep understanding of human cognition.
- The ability to replicate creativity, emotions, and intuition.
- Ethical considerations about creating machines with human-like consciousness.

While General AI remains a goal for the future, it's still largely in the realm of science fiction—for now.

---

3. Superintelligence: Beyond Human Capabilities

Superintelligence refers to AI that surpasses human intelligence in every way. This concept takes General AI a step further, imagining machines that:

- **Outperform Humans:** They could solve problems we can't, invent new technologies, and make decisions faster and more accurately.

- **Self-Improve:** A superintelligent AI could improve its own design, leading to rapid advancements beyond human control.
- **Existential Questions:** Superintelligence raises profound ethical and philosophical questions. Would it be a force for good, or could it pose risks to humanity?

The Debate Around Superintelligence

Some experts, like Elon Musk and Stephen Hawking, have warned about the potential dangers of superintelligent AI. Others, like Ray Kurzweil, are optimistic, believing it could help solve humanity's biggest challenges, such as climate change and disease.

How Do These Types of AI Compare?

Here's a quick summary of the three types of AI:

Type of AI	Capabilities	Examples	Status
Narrow AI	Performs specific tasks	Siri, Netflix recommendations	Widely used today
General AI	Thinks and reasons like a human	None yet (still theoretical)	Not yet achieved
Superintelligence	Surpasses human intelligence in all areas	None (exists only in theory/fiction)	Speculative and futuristic

Why Does This Matter?

Understanding the different types of AI helps you:

- **Appreciate Current Technology:** Recognize the power and limitations of the AI tools you use every day.
- **Think About the Future:** Consider the possibilities and challenges of more advanced AI systems.
- **Engage in Ethical Discussions:** Participate in conversations about how AI should be developed and used responsibly.

What's Next?

While Narrow AI is already transforming our world, General AI and Superintelligence remain exciting—and sometimes controversial—topics for the future. As we continue to advance AI technology, it's important to stay informed and think critically about its impact on society.

5. AI in Everyday Life: Applications You Already Use

Artificial Intelligence isn't just a futuristic concept—it's already here, making our lives easier, more efficient, and even more fun. From the moment you wake up to the time you go to bed, AI is working behind the scenes to enhance your day. In this chapter, we'll explore some of the most common ways AI is used in everyday life.

---

1. Smartphones: Your Pocket-Sized AI Assistant

Your smartphone is packed with AI-powered features that you probably use every day:
- **Voice Assistants:** Siri, Google Assistant, and Alexa use natural language processing (NLP) to understand your voice commands and respond intelligently.
- **Camera Enhancements:** AI improves your photos by adjusting lighting, detecting faces, and even suggesting the best shots.
- **Predictive Text:** When your keyboard suggests the next word you're about to type, that's AI at work.

---

2. Social Media: Curating Your Online Experience

Social media platforms rely heavily on AI to keep you engaged:
- **Content Recommendations:** AI algorithms analyze your behavior to show you posts, videos, and ads tailored to your interests.
- **Face Recognition:** Platforms like Facebook use AI to tag people in photos automatically.
- **Moderation:** AI helps detect and remove harmful content, such as hate speech or fake news.

---

3. Streaming Services: Your Personal Entertainment Guru

Ever wonder how Netflix always knows what you want to watch? That's AI:
- **Recommendation Systems:** AI analyzes your viewing history to suggest movies and TV shows you might like.
- **Content Creation:** Some platforms use AI to generate personalized trailers or even create original content.

---

4. Online Shopping: The AI-Powered Marketplace

AI is transforming the way we shop online:
- **Product Recommendations:** Amazon and other e-commerce sites use AI to suggest products based on your browsing and purchase history.

- **Virtual Try-Ons:** Some apps use AI to let you "try on" clothes, glasses, or makeup virtually.
- **Customer Support:** Chatbots powered by AI can answer your questions and help you resolve issues quickly.

5. Navigation and Travel: Getting You Where You Need to Go

AI makes travel and navigation smoother and more efficient:
- **GPS Apps:** Google Maps and Waze use AI to analyze traffic patterns and suggest the fastest routes.
- **Ride-Sharing:** Apps like Uber and Lyft use AI to match drivers with passengers and optimize routes.
- **Travel Planning:** AI-powered tools can help you find the best flights, hotels, and activities based on your preferences.

6. Healthcare: AI as Your Health Ally

AI is playing an increasingly important role in healthcare:
- **Diagnostics:** AI systems can analyze medical images (like X-rays and MRIs) to detect diseases such as cancer.
- **Wearables:** Devices like Fitbit and Apple Watch use AI to monitor your health metrics and provide personalized insights.
- **Virtual Health Assistants:** AI chatbots can answer health-related questions and remind you to take your medication.

7. Banking and Finance: Smarter Money Management

AI is revolutionizing the way we handle money:
- **Fraud Detection:** Banks use AI to monitor transactions and detect suspicious activity.
- **Personalized Financial Advice:** Apps like Mint and Robinhood use AI to provide budgeting tips and investment recommendations.
- **Customer Service:** AI-powered chatbots can help you check your balance, transfer funds, and more.

8. Smart Homes: Living in the Future

AI is making our homes smarter and more convenient:
- **Smart Speakers:** Devices like Amazon Echo and Google Nest use AI to control your lights, thermostat, and appliances with voice commands.
- **Security Systems:** AI-powered cameras can recognize faces and alert you to unusual activity.
- **Energy Efficiency:** AI can optimize your home's energy usage, saving you money and reducing your carbon footprint.

9. Creative Tools: Unleashing Your Inner Artist

AI is even making its way into the creative world:
- **Art and Music:** Tools like DALL·E and AIVA use AI to generate art and compose music.
- **Writing Assistants:** AI-powered tools like Grammarly help you write better by suggesting improvements and catching errors.
- **Video Editing:** AI can automatically edit videos, add effects, and even generate captions.

---

10. Gaming: A Smarter Playground

AI is enhancing the gaming experience in exciting ways:
- **NPCs (Non-Player Characters):** AI makes in-game characters more realistic and responsive.
- **Personalized Gameplay:** AI adjusts the difficulty level based on your skills and preferences.
- **Game Development:** AI can help developers create more immersive and dynamic game worlds.

Now we can see a lot of research and innovations using AI, e.g, discovering Drug, counting elephants, generating 3D holograms in real-time, detecting powdery mildew easily, analyzing satellite images, thought-to-speech system, improving the prediction of stroke recovery, fighting disinformation, teaching robots to make appropriate reactive human facial expressions, Diagnose Skin Conditions, Driverless Ride-Hailing Services, pinpoint Local Pollution Hotspots, explore the biomolecular world, Telehealth, speed up drug development, improving vaccine delivery, and many other things.

Though we already started getting the benefits of AI, still various AI-related research are going on. For example, researchers are trying hard to develop **Generic AI** which can be used in any field. Personally, I witnessed the power of AI while running my YouTube channel. Previously I used to spend a lot of time and effort for creating subtitles/captions for my videos. Now, it can be done very easily without spending any time or effort. It is possible because of the AI which is improved a lot to understand anyone's voice and transcribe it automatically.

I believe Quantum computing developments will further increase the usage and growth of AI.

People are afraid that AI will grab the job opportunities of them. Though it may not happen overnight, surely AI will affect the job market heavily in the long run. That's why Governments are working on Universal Basic Income schemes.

List of AI Tools to Explore

- ◆ **AI Chatbots & Assistants**
1. ChatGPT (OpenAI)

A powerful AI chatbot for writing, coding, brainstorming, and more.

2. Gemini (Google AI)

Google's AI assistant that integrates with Google Search and Workspace.

3. Perplexity AI

An AI-powered search engine that provides cited sources for reliable answers.

■ Try This: Ask ChatGPT to summarize a complex topic or help write a blog post!

- **AI for Image Generation & Editing**
4. DALL·E (OpenAI)

Generates stunning AI-created images from text prompts.

5. Canva AI (Magic Design, Magic Edit)

An AI-powered design tool for creating professional graphics easily.

6. Remove.bg

Instantly removes backgrounds from images with AI.

■ Try This: Generate an AI artwork with DALL·E or remove a background in seconds!

- **AI for Video Creation**
7. Runway ML

A powerful AI tool for text-to-video generation and video editing.

8. Synthesia

Create videos using AI-generated avatars and voiceovers.

9. Pika Labs

Turn text descriptions into AI-generated animations.

■ Try This: Generate an AI explainer video using Synthesia!

- **AI for Audio & Voice**
10. ElevenLabs

A high-quality AI voice generator for lifelike speech.

11. Whisper (OpenAI)

An AI-powered speech-to-text transcription tool.

12. Voicify AI

Clone and modify voices using AI.

◼ Try This: Convert text into an AI-generated voice using ElevenLabs!

• **AI for Code & Development**

13. GitHub Copilot

An AI coding assistant that helps write code faster.

14. Codeium

A free AI-powered alternative to GitHub Copilot.

15. Tabnine

AI-powered code suggestions for developers.

◼ Try This: Use GitHub Copilot to autocomplete a Python function!

• **AI for Productivity**

16. Notion AI

An AI-powered assistant inside Notion for writing and summarization.

17. Otter.ai

AI transcription tool for meetings and lectures.

18. Grammarly AI

An AI-powered writing assistant for error-free content.

◼ Try This: Use Notion AI to summarize a long document instantly!

• **AI for Research & Learning**

19. Elicit.org

An AI-powered research assistant that summarizes academic papers.

20. Scite.ai

An AI tool that verifies claims in research papers.

21. Consensus AI

Finds research-backed answers using AI.

■ Try This: Use Elicit to summarize a research paper in seconds!

---

* **Fun AI Experiments**
22. This Person Does Not Exist

Generates AI-created faces of non-existent people.

23. Deep Nostalgia

Animates old photos using AI.

24. AI Dungeon

An AI-powered text-based adventure game.

■ Try This: Generate a fictional AI-created face and write a story about them using ChatGPT!

AI tools are evolving rapidly, offering endless possibilities for creativity, productivity, and automation. Whether you're looking to enhance your workflow, create stunning visuals, or explore AI-generated content, these tools can help you get started!

Why Does This Matter?
Understanding how AI is used in everyday life helps you:
- **Appreciate Its Impact:** Recognize how AI is making your life easier and more enjoyable.
- **Make Informed Choices:** Be aware of the tools and services you use and how they leverage AI.
- **Stay Curious:** Explore new AI-powered technologies and see how they can benefit you.

What's Next?
As AI continues to evolve, its applications will only become more widespread and sophisticated. From smart cities to personalized education, the possibilities are endless. In the next chapter, we'll dive deeper into the heart of AI: **Machine Learning**.

6. Machine Learning: The Heart of AI

If Artificial Intelligence is the brain, then Machine Learning (ML) is the heart that keeps it beating. Machine Learning is the technology that enables AI systems to learn from data, improve over time, and make intelligent decisions. In this chapter, we'll explore what machine learning is, how it works, and why it's so important.

What is Machine Learning?

Machine Learning is a subset of AI that focuses on teaching computers to learn from data and make predictions or decisions without being explicitly programmed. Instead of following rigid instructions, ML systems identify patterns in data and use them to improve their performance. Think of it like teaching a child:

- You show them examples (data).
- They learn from those examples (training).
- Over time, they get better at recognizing patterns and making decisions (improvement).

How Does Machine Learning Work?

Machine Learning involves three key steps:

1. **Data Collection:**
   The first step is gathering data. This could be anything from customer purchase histories to medical records or even images of cats and dogs.
2. **Training the Model:**
   The data is fed into an algorithm, which analyzes it to find patterns. For example, if you're training a model to recognize cats, you'd show it thousands of pictures of cats and non-cats.
3. **Testing and Improving:**
   Once trained, the model is tested on new data to see how well it performs. If it makes mistakes, it's adjusted and trained again. This process continues until the model achieves the desired accuracy.

Types of Machine Learning

There are three main types of machine learning, each with its own approach:

1. **Supervised Learning**
   - The AI is given labeled data (e.g., pictures of cats labeled "cat" and pictures of dogs labeled "dog").
   - It learns to map inputs to the correct outputs.
   - Example: A spam filter that learns to classify emails as "spam" or "not spam."
2. **Unsupervised Learning**
   - The AI is given unlabeled data and must find patterns on its own.
   - Example: Grouping customers into segments based on their shopping behavior.
3. **Reinforcement Learning**

- The AI learns by trial and error, receiving rewards for good actions and penalties for bad ones.
- Example: Training a robot to walk or a computer program to play a game.

Real-World Applications of Machine Learning

Machine Learning is behind many of the technologies we use every day. Here are some examples:

- **Recommendation Systems:** Netflix and Spotify use ML to suggest movies and music you might like.
- **Image and Speech Recognition:** Facebook uses ML to tag people in photos, and voice assistants like Siri use it to understand your voice commands.
- **Healthcare:** ML helps doctors diagnose diseases by analyzing medical images.
- **Finance:** Banks use ML to detect fraudulent transactions and assess credit risk.

Why is Machine Learning Important?

Machine Learning is the driving force behind many AI advancements because:

- **It Enables Automation:** ML allows machines to perform tasks that would otherwise require human intelligence.
- **It Improves Over Time:** Unlike traditional software, ML systems get better with more data and experience.
- **It Solves Complex Problems:** ML can analyze vast amounts of data to find patterns and insights that humans might miss.

Challenges in Machine Learning

While ML is powerful, it's not without its challenges:

- **Data Quality:** ML models are only as good as the data they're trained on. Poor-quality data can lead to inaccurate results.
- **Bias:** If the training data is biased, the model's predictions will be too. For example, a facial recognition system trained mostly on one ethnicity might struggle with others.
- **Computational Resources:** Training ML models requires significant computing power, which can be expensive and energy-intensive.

The Future of Machine Learning

As technology advances, Machine Learning is becoming more accessible and powerful. Here are some trends to watch:

- **Automated Machine Learning (AutoML):** Tools that make it easier for non-experts to build ML models.
- **Edge AI:** Running ML models on devices (like smartphones) instead of in the cloud, for faster and more private processing.
- **Ethical AI:** Efforts to ensure ML systems are fair, transparent, and accountable.

Why Should You Care About Machine Learning?

Understanding Machine Learning helps you:
- **Appreciate the Technology You Use:** Recognize the ML behind your favorite apps and services.
- **Stay Informed:** Keep up with advancements that are shaping the future.
- **Explore Opportunities:** Whether you're a student, professional, or hobbyist, ML offers exciting opportunities to learn and innovate.

What's Next?

Now that you understand the basics of Machine Learning, let's explore the fuel that powers it: **Data**. In the next chapter, we'll dive into the importance of data in AI and how it's collected, processed, and used.

7. Data: The Fuel That Powers AI

Imagine building a car without fuel—it might look impressive, but it won't go anywhere. The same is true for Artificial Intelligence. Without data, AI systems can't learn, improve, or make decisions. In this chapter, we'll explore why data is the lifeblood of AI, how it's used, and the challenges that come with it.

Why is Data So Important?

Data is the foundation of AI. Here's why:
- **Learning from Examples:** AI systems learn by analyzing data. The more data they have, the better they can identify patterns and make accurate predictions.
- **Improving Over Time:** As AI systems process more data, they refine their models and become more effective.
- **Enabling Personalization:** Data allows AI to tailor experiences to individual users, like recommending movies or suggesting products.

Without data, AI would be like a student without textbooks—unable to learn or grow.

Types of Data

Data comes in many forms, and each type is useful for different AI applications:
1. **Structured Data:**
    - Organized and easy to analyze (e.g., spreadsheets, databases).
    - Example: Customer purchase histories used for product recommendations.
2. **Unstructured Data:**
    - Not organized in a predefined way (e.g., text, images, videos).
    - Example: Social media posts analyzed for sentiment or trends.
3. **Semi-Structured Data:**

- A mix of structured and unstructured data (e.g., emails, XML files).
- Example: Email headers (structured) combined with the body text (unstructured).

How is Data Collected?

Data is gathered from a variety of sources, including:
- **User Input:** Information provided by users, such as search queries or survey responses.
- **Sensors and Devices:** Data from smartphones, wearables, and IoT devices (e.g., fitness trackers, smart thermostats).
- **Public Datasets:** Open-source datasets available for research and development.
- **Web Scraping:** Extracting data from websites for analysis.

The Data Pipeline: From Raw Data to Insights

Before data can be used by AI systems, it goes through several steps:
1. **Collection:** Gathering raw data from various sources.
2. **Cleaning:** Removing errors, duplicates, and irrelevant information.
3. **Processing:** Organizing and transforming data into a usable format.
4. **Analysis:** Using algorithms to extract patterns and insights.
5. **Storage:** Storing data securely for future use.

Challenges with Data

While data is essential, working with it isn't always easy. Here are some common challenges:
- **Quality:** Poor-quality data (e.g., incomplete, outdated, or inaccurate) can lead to flawed AI models.
- **Bias:** If the data reflects human biases, the AI system will too. For example, a hiring algorithm trained on biased data might favor certain demographics.
- **Privacy:** Collecting and using personal data raises concerns about privacy and security.
- **Volume:** The sheer amount of data generated every day can be overwhelming to process and store.

Big Data and AI

The term "Big Data" refers to extremely large datasets that are too complex for traditional data processing tools. AI thrives on Big Data because:
- **More Data = Better Models:** With more data, AI systems can identify subtle patterns and make more accurate predictions.
- **Real-Time Processing:** AI can analyze Big Data in real time, enabling applications like fraud detection and live traffic updates.

Ethical Considerations

As AI relies more on data, ethical questions arise:

- **Ownership:** Who owns the data—the user, the company collecting it, or both?
- **Consent:** Are users aware of how their data is being used, and have they agreed to it?
- **Transparency:** Are AI systems making decisions in a way that's understandable and fair?

Why Should You Care About Data?

Understanding the role of data in AI helps you:
- **Make Informed Choices:** Be aware of how your data is used and take steps to protect your privacy.
- **Spot Potential Issues:** Recognize when data might be biased or misused.
- **Appreciate the Complexity:** Gain a deeper understanding of what makes AI systems work.

What's Next?

Now that you know how important data is to AI, let's explore the ethical implications of this powerful technology. In the next chapter, we'll dive into **Ethical AI: The Good, the Bad, and the Ugly**.

8. Ethical AI: The Good, the Bad, and the Ugly

Artificial Intelligence has the power to transform our world for the better, but it also raises important ethical questions. From bias in algorithms to privacy concerns, the ethical implications of AI are complex and far-reaching. In this chapter, we'll explore the good, the bad, and the ugly sides of AI, and why it's crucial to develop and use this technology responsibly.

The Good: How AI is Making the World Better

AI has the potential to solve some of humanity's biggest challenges and improve our lives in countless ways:
- **Healthcare:** AI is helping doctors diagnose diseases earlier and more accurately, leading to better patient outcomes.
- **Education:** AI-powered tools are personalizing learning experiences, making education more accessible and effective.
- **Environment:** AI is being used to monitor climate change, optimize energy usage, and protect endangered species.
- **Accessibility:** AI is breaking down barriers for people with disabilities, from speech-to-text tools to smart prosthetics.

These examples show how AI can be a force for good, creating a more equitable and sustainable world.

The Bad: Challenges and Risks of AI

Despite its potential, AI also comes with significant challenges and risks:

1. **Bias in AI Systems**
   - AI models are only as good as the data they're trained on. If the data is biased, the AI will be too.
   - Example: A hiring algorithm trained on biased data might favor certain demographics, perpetuating inequality.
2. **Privacy Concerns**
   - AI systems often rely on personal data, raising questions about how that data is collected, stored, and used.
   - Example: Facial recognition technology can be used for surveillance, potentially infringing on individual privacy.
3. **Job Displacement**
   - Automation powered by AI could replace certain jobs, leading to economic disruption and inequality.
   - Example: Self-driving trucks might reduce the need for human drivers, impacting millions of jobs.
4. **Lack of Transparency**
   - Many AI systems operate as "black boxes," making it difficult to understand how they arrive at their decisions.
   - Example: If an AI system denies a loan application, the applicant might not know why.

The Ugly: Potential for Harm

In some cases, AI can be misused or have unintended consequences:

- **Weaponization:** AI could be used to develop autonomous weapons, raising ethical and security concerns.
- **Deepfakes:** AI-generated fake videos and audio can spread misinformation and damage reputations.
- **Surveillance States:** Governments could use AI to monitor and control citizens, eroding freedoms and human rights.

Principles of Ethical AI

To address these challenges, many organizations are developing principles for ethical AI. These include:

1. **Fairness:** Ensuring AI systems are free from bias and treat all users equitably.
2. **Transparency:** Making AI decision-making processes understandable and explainable.
3. **Accountability:** Holding developers and organizations responsible for the impact of their AI systems.
4. **Privacy:** Protecting user data and ensuring it's used responsibly.
5. **Safety:** Designing AI systems that are secure and reliable.

The Role of Regulation

Governments and organizations are beginning to regulate AI to ensure it's used ethically. Examples include:

- **GDPR (General Data Protection Regulation):** A European law that protects user data and privacy.
- **AI Ethics Guidelines:** Frameworks developed by organizations like the IEEE and the Partnership on AI to promote responsible AI development.

Why Should You Care About Ethical AI?

Understanding the ethical implications of AI is important because:

- **It Affects Everyone:** AI impacts our lives in ways big and small, from the apps we use to the jobs we have.
- **It Shapes the Future:** The choices we make today will determine how AI evolves and how it's used in the future.
- **It's a Shared Responsibility:** Everyone—developers, businesses, governments, and users—has a role to play in ensuring AI is used ethically.

What's Next?

Now that we've explored the ethical dimensions of AI, let's shift our focus to the tools and platforms that make AI accessible to everyone. In the next chapter, we'll dive into **AI Tools and Platforms for Beginners**.

9. AI Tools and Platforms for Beginners

You don't need to be a computer scientist or a coding expert to start exploring Artificial Intelligence. Thanks to a wide range of user-friendly tools and platforms, anyone can dive into the world of AI. In this chapter, we'll introduce you to some of the best tools and platforms for beginners, whether you're looking to learn, experiment, or build your own AI projects.

Why Use AI Tools and Platforms?

AI tools and platforms are designed to simplify the process of working with AI. They offer:

- **Ease of Use:** Many tools have drag-and-drop interfaces or require little to no coding.
- **Accessibility:** They make AI accessible to non-experts, including students, hobbyists, and professionals.
- **Pre-Built Models:** Some platforms provide ready-to-use AI models, so you don't have to start from scratch.
- **Learning Resources:** Many tools come with tutorials, documentation, and community support to help you get started.

Top AI Tools and Platforms for Beginners

Here are some of the most popular and beginner-friendly AI tools and platforms:

---

1. Google Teachable Machine

- **What It Is:** A web-based tool that lets you create machine learning models without coding.
- **What You Can Do:** Train models to recognize images, sounds, or poses using your own data.
- **Why It's Great for Beginners:** It's free, easy to use, and requires no prior experience.

---

2. TensorFlow Playground

- **What It Is:** An interactive web application that helps you understand how neural networks work.
- **What You Can Do:** Experiment with different parameters and see how they affect the model's performance.
- **Why It's Great for Beginners:** It's a fun and visual way to learn the basics of machine learning.

---

3. IBM Watson Studio

- **What It Is:** A cloud-based platform for building and deploying AI models.
- **What You Can Do:** Use pre-built models, create your own, and collaborate with others.
- **Why It's Great for Beginners:** It offers a free tier and plenty of tutorials to get you started.

---

4. Microsoft Azure Machine Learning

- **What It Is:** A cloud-based service for building, training, and deploying machine learning models.
- **What You Can Do:** Use drag-and-drop tools to create models or write code in Python or R.
- **Why It's Great for Beginners:** It integrates with other Microsoft tools and offers a free tier.

---

5. Runway ML

- **What It Is:** A creative toolkit for artists, designers, and creators to use AI in their projects.
- **What You Can Do:** Generate art, edit videos, and create music using AI models.
- **Why It's Great for Beginners:** It's designed for non-technical users and offers a free plan.

---

6. Hugging Face

- **What It Is:** A platform for natural language processing (NLP) models.
- **What You Can Do:** Use pre-trained models for tasks like text generation, translation, and sentiment analysis.
- **Why It's Great for Beginners:** It's free to use and has a large community of users and developers. Hugging Face's transformers library stands as a powerhouse, offering state-of-the-art pretrained models that can handle a wide range of tasks. At the heart of its simplicity and power lies the pipeline API, an intuitive interface that abstracts away the complexities of model loading, tokenization, and inference, allowing developers and data scientists to focus on building impactful applications.

---

7. AutoML by Google Cloud

- **What It Is:** A suite of tools that automates the process of building machine learning models.
- **What You Can Do:** Train high-quality models with minimal effort and expertise.
- **Why It's Great for Beginners:** It simplifies the process of creating custom models.

How to Choose the Right Tool

With so many options available, how do you choose the right tool for your needs? Here are some factors to consider:

- **Your Goals:** Are you looking to learn, experiment, or build a specific project?
- **Ease of Use:** Do you prefer a no-code platform or are you comfortable with some coding?
- **Cost:** Are you looking for free tools or are you willing to pay for advanced features?
- **Community and Support:** Does the tool have a strong community and good documentation?

Getting Started with AI Tools

Here's a simple roadmap to get started with AI tools:

1. **Explore:** Try out a few tools to see which one you like best.
2. **Learn:** Use tutorials and documentation to understand how the tool works.
3. **Experiment:** Start with small projects to build your confidence.
4. **Share:** Join online communities to share your work and learn from others.

Why Should You Care About AI Tools?

Using AI tools and platforms can help you:

- **Learn New Skills:** Gain hands-on experience with AI, even if you're not a programmer.
- **Unlock Creativity:** Use AI to create art, music, and other creative projects.
- **Solve Problems:** Build AI solutions for real-world challenges.
- **Stay Ahead:** Stay informed about the latest advancements in AI.

What's Next?

Now that you know about the tools and platforms available, let's explore how you can turn your interest in AI into a career. In the next chapter, we'll dive into **AI Careers: How to Start Your Journey in AI**.

10. AI Careers: How to Start Your Journey in AI

Artificial Intelligence is one of the most exciting and fast-growing fields today. Whether you're a student, a professional looking to switch careers, or simply curious about AI, there's never been a better time to explore opportunities in this field. In this chapter, we'll walk you through the steps to start your journey in AI, the skills you'll need, and the career paths you can pursue.

Why Pursue a Career in AI?

AI is transforming industries and creating new opportunities. Here's why a career in AI is worth considering:

- **High Demand:** AI professionals are in high demand across industries, from healthcare to finance to entertainment.
- **Competitive Salaries:** AI roles often come with attractive salaries and benefits.
- **Impactful Work:** AI allows you to work on cutting-edge technologies that can solve real-world problems.
- **Continuous Learning:** The field is constantly evolving, offering endless opportunities to learn and grow.

Key Skills for a Career in AI

To succeed in AI, you'll need a mix of technical and soft skills. Here's a breakdown:

1. Technical Skills

- **Programming:** Learn languages like Python, R, or Java, which are widely used in AI development.
- **Mathematics:** A strong foundation in linear algebra, calculus, and probability is essential for understanding AI algorithms.
- **Machine Learning:** Familiarize yourself with machine learning concepts, tools, and frameworks like TensorFlow and PyTorch.
- **Data Analysis:** Learn how to collect, clean, and analyze data using tools like Pandas and NumPy.
- **Big Data:** Understand how to work with large datasets using tools like Hadoop and Spark.

2. Soft Skills

- **Problem-Solving:** AI professionals need to think critically and come up with innovative solutions.
- **Communication:** You'll often need to explain complex concepts to non-technical stakeholders.
- **Collaboration:** AI projects often involve working in teams with diverse skill sets.
- **Curiosity:** A willingness to learn and explore new ideas is crucial in this fast-evolving field.

Career Paths in AI

AI offers a wide range of career options. Here are some of the most popular roles:

1. Data Scientist

- **What They Do:** Analyze data to extract insights and build predictive models.
- **Skills Needed:** Data analysis, machine learning, programming, and statistics.

2. Machine Learning Engineer

- **What They Do:** Design and implement machine learning systems and algorithms.
- **Skills Needed:** Machine learning, programming, and software engineering.

3. AI Research Scientist

- **What They Do:** Conduct research to develop new AI algorithms and techniques.
- **Skills Needed:** Advanced mathematics, machine learning, and research skills.

4. AI Ethics Consultant

- **What They Do:** Ensure AI systems are developed and used ethically and responsibly.
- **Skills Needed:** Ethics, law, and AI knowledge.

5. AI Product Manager

- **What They Do:** Oversee the development and deployment of AI-powered products.
- **Skills Needed:** Project management, AI knowledge, and communication.

6. Robotics Engineer

- **What They Do:** Design and build robots that use AI to perform tasks.
- **Skills Needed:** Robotics, programming, and machine learning.

How to Get Started in AI

Here's a step-by-step guide to kickstart your AI career:

1. Learn the Basics
- Take online courses or read books to understand the fundamentals of AI and machine learning.
- Platforms like Coursera, edX, and Udacity offer beginner-friendly courses.

2. Build Your Skills
- Practice coding and work on small projects to apply what you've learned.
- Participate in online competitions like Kaggle to hone your skills.

3. Get Certified
- Earn certifications in AI, machine learning, or data science to boost your resume.
- Popular certifications include Google's TensorFlow Developer Certificate and IBM's AI Engineering Professional Certificate.

4. Build a Portfolio
- Showcase your skills by creating a portfolio of projects. This could include anything from a simple chatbot to a machine learning model that predicts housing prices.

5. Network
- Join AI communities, attend conferences, and connect with professionals in the field.
- Platforms like LinkedIn and Meetup are great for networking.

6. Apply for Jobs
- Start applying for entry-level positions or internships in AI.
- Tailor your resume and cover letter to highlight your skills and projects.

Resources for Learning AI
Here are some resources to help you get started:
- **Online Courses:** Coursera, edX, Udacity, and Khan Academy.
- **Communities:** Kaggle, GitHub, and AI-focused forums like Reddit's r/MachineLearning.

Why Should You Care About an AI Career?
Pursuing a career in AI can open doors to exciting opportunities and allow you to make a meaningful impact. Whether you're passionate about technology, problem-solving, or innovation, AI offers a rewarding and dynamic career path.

What's Next?

Now that you know how to start your journey in AI, let's explore some fun and practical projects you can try at home. In the next chapter, we'll dive into **Fun AI Projects to Try at Home**.

11. Fun AI Projects to Try at Home

One of the best ways to learn about AI is by doing. In this chapter, we'll explore some fun and easy AI projects you can try at home, even if you're a beginner. These projects will help you understand how AI works, build your skills, and spark your creativity. Let's get started!

Why Try AI Projects at Home?

Working on AI projects at home allows you to:

- **Learn by Doing:** Apply theoretical knowledge to practical problems.
- **Build Confidence:** Gain hands-on experience and see your ideas come to life.
- **Explore Creativity:** Use AI to create art, music, games, and more.
- **Prepare for a Career:** Build a portfolio of projects to showcase your skills.

Project 1: Build a Simple Chatbot

What You'll Learn: Natural Language Processing (NLP) and conversational AI.
Tools Needed: Python, libraries like NLTK or ChatterBot.
Steps:

1. Install Python and the ChatterBot or Rasa library.
2. Train your chatbot using a dataset or pre-built models.
3. Customize your chatbot's responses and test it in a conversation.

Why It's Fun: You can create a chatbot that talks like your favorite character or helps with simple tasks like answering FAQs.

Project 2: Create an Image Recognition App

What You'll Learn: Computer vision and image classification.
Tools Needed: Google Teachable Machine or TensorFlow.
Steps:

1. Use Google Teachable Machine to upload and label images (e.g., cats vs. dogs).
2. Train your model and export it.
3. Integrate the model into a simple app or website.

Why It's Fun: You can create an app that recognizes objects, animals, or even your friends' faces.

Project 3: Generate Art with AI

What You'll Learn: Generative AI and creative applications of AI.

Tools Needed: Runway ML or DeepArt.io.

Steps:

1. Upload an image to a generative AI tool.
2. Apply different styles or let the AI create something new.
3. Download and share your AI-generated artwork.

Why It's Fun: You can create unique pieces of art and even print them to decorate your home.

Project 4: Build a Music Recommendation System

What You'll Learn: Recommendation systems and data analysis.

Tools Needed: Python, libraries like Pandas and Scikit-learn.

Steps:

1. Collect a dataset of songs and user preferences.
2. Use a machine learning algorithm to analyze the data.
3. Build a system that recommends songs based on user input.

Why It's Fun: You can create your own version of Spotify's recommendation engine.

Project 5: Train a Game-Playing AI

What You'll Learn: Reinforcement learning and game AI.

Tools Needed: Python, libraries like Pygame and TensorFlow.

Steps:

1. Choose a simple game (e.g., Tic-Tac-Toe or Snake).
2. Use reinforcement learning to train an AI to play the game.
3. Watch your AI improve over time.

Why It's Fun: You can challenge your AI to a game and see if you can beat it.

Project 6: Create a Sentiment Analysis Tool

What You'll Learn: Text analysis and sentiment classification.

Tools Needed: Python, libraries like TextBlob or VADER.

Steps:

1. Collect text data (e.g., tweets or product reviews).
2. Use a sentiment analysis tool to classify the text as positive, negative, or neutral.
3. Visualize the results using graphs or charts.

Why It's Fun: You can analyze social media trends or see how people feel about your favorite products.

Project 7: Build a Voice Assistant

What You'll Learn: Speech recognition and voice-based AI.

Tools Needed: Python, libraries like SpeechRecognition and PyAudio.

Steps:

1. Set up a speech recognition system to understand voice commands.
2. Add functionality like answering questions or controlling smart devices.
3. Customize your assistant's personality and responses.

Why It's Fun: You can create your own version of Siri or Alexa.

Tips for Success

- **Start Small:** Begin with simple projects and gradually take on more complex challenges.
- **Experiment:** Don't be afraid to try new ideas and make mistakes.
- **Share Your Work:** Share your projects with friends, online communities, or on social media to get feedback and inspire others.

Why Should You Try AI Projects at Home?

Working on AI projects at home helps you:

- **Gain Practical Experience:** Apply what you've learned in a hands-on way.
- **Build a Portfolio:** Showcase your projects to potential employers or collaborators.
- **Have Fun:** Explore your creativity and discover new passions.

What's Next?

Now that you've explored some fun AI projects, let's look ahead to the future of AI. In the next chapter, we'll dive into **The Future of AI: What's Next?**

12. The Future of AI: What's Next?

Artificial Intelligence has come a long way, but the journey is far from over. As technology continues to evolve, AI is poised to transform our world in ways we can only begin to imagine. In this chapter, we'll explore the future of AI, from emerging trends to the ethical and societal challenges that lie ahead.

Emerging Trends in AI

The field of AI is constantly evolving. Here are some of the most exciting trends to watch:

---

1. Generative AI

- **What It Is:** AI systems that can create new content, such as text, images, music, and even videos.
- **Examples:** Tools like ChatGPT, DALL·E, and MidJourney.
- **Impact:** Generative AI is revolutionizing creative industries, from art and design to marketing and entertainment.

---

2. Edge AI

- **What It Is:** Running AI algorithms directly on devices (like smartphones and IoT devices) instead of in the cloud.
- **Examples:** Smart home devices, autonomous drones, and wearable health monitors.
- **Impact:** Edge AI enables faster processing, greater privacy, and real-time decision-making.

3. AI in Healthcare

- **What It Is:** Using AI to improve diagnosis, treatment, and patient care.
- **Examples:** AI-powered diagnostic tools, personalized medicine, and robotic surgery.
- **Impact:** AI has the potential to make healthcare more accurate, efficient, and accessible.

4. Autonomous Systems

- **What It Is:** AI-powered systems that can operate without human intervention.
- **Examples:** Self-driving cars, delivery drones, and smart factories.
- **Impact:** Autonomous systems could transform transportation, logistics, and manufacturing.

5. AI and Climate Change

- **What It Is:** Using AI to address environmental challenges.
- **Examples:** Optimizing energy usage, monitoring deforestation, and predicting natural disasters.
- **Impact:** AI could play a crucial role in combating climate change and promoting sustainability.

The Road to General AI

While Narrow AI (focused on specific tasks) is already widespread, the dream of General AI (machines with human-like intelligence) remains a long-term goal. Here's what the journey might look like:

- **Current State:** AI systems excel at specific tasks but lack common sense and adaptability.
- **Challenges:** Developing AI that can understand context, reason, and learn across domains.
- **Potential:** General AI could revolutionize fields like science, education, and creativity.

Ethical and Societal Challenges

As AI continues to advance, it raises important ethical and societal questions:

- **Bias and Fairness:** How can we ensure AI systems are fair and unbiased?
- **Privacy:** How do we protect personal data in an AI-driven world?

- **Job Displacement:** How can we prepare for the impact of AI on employment?
- **Regulation:** What rules and guidelines are needed to ensure AI is used responsibly?

The Role of Collaboration

The future of AI will depend on collaboration between:
- **Researchers:** Pushing the boundaries of what AI can do.
- **Governments:** Creating policies and regulations to guide AI development.
- **Businesses:** Developing and deploying AI solutions responsibly.
- **Society:** Engaging in conversations about how AI should be used.

Why Should You Care About the Future of AI?

Understanding the future of AI helps you:
- **Stay Informed:** Keep up with advancements that could impact your life and career.
- **Be Prepared:** Anticipate changes and adapt to new opportunities and challenges.
- **Make a Difference:** Contribute to shaping the future of AI in a positive and ethical way.

What's Next?

As we wrap up this ebook, let's revisit some of the key takeaways and explore how you can continue your journey into the world of AI. In the final chapter, we'll provide a **Conclusion and Next Steps**.

13. Frequently Asked Questions (FAQ)

1. AI Basics

Q: What is AI, and how does it work?
A: AI (Artificial Intelligence) is the simulation of human intelligence in machines. It works by processing data, recognizing patterns, and making decisions based on algorithms and models.

Q: What's the difference between AI, Machine Learning, and Deep Learning?
A: AI is the broad field of creating intelligent systems. Machine Learning (ML) is a subset of AI that enables machines to learn from data without explicit programming. Deep Learning is a further subset of ML that uses neural networks to process large amounts of data.

Q: Is AI the same as automation?
A: No, automation follows predefined rules, while AI learns and adapts to new information to improve performance.

Q: Can AI become smarter than humans?
A: AI can outperform humans in specific tasks, but it lacks general intelligence, creativity, and

emotions that make human intelligence unique.

2. AI in Daily Life

Q: How does AI impact everyday life?
A: AI is present in search engines, recommendation systems (Netflix, YouTube), virtual assistants (Alexa, Siri), fraud detection, medical diagnostics, and more.

Q: Is AI dangerous? Will it take my job?
A: AI can automate repetitive tasks, but it also creates new job opportunities. The key is to learn AI-related skills to stay relevant in the evolving job market.

Q: Can AI think like a human?
A: No, AI processes information and makes decisions based on algorithms, but it lacks consciousness, emotions, and true understanding.

Q: Does AI have biases?
A: Yes, AI models can have biases based on the data they are trained on. Ensuring diverse and fair datasets can help mitigate bias.

3. Learning & Career in AI

Q: Do I need coding skills to learn AI?
A: Not necessarily. Many AI tools allow users to build models without coding. However, learning Python can help in advanced AI development.

Q: What programming languages are best for AI?
A: Python is the most popular language for AI, followed by R, Java, and Julia.

Q: How long does it take to learn AI?
A: It depends on your background. A beginner can learn the basics in a few months, while mastering AI may take years.

Q: What industries use AI the most?
A: Healthcare, finance, retail, automotive, and cybersecurity are among the top industries integrating AI solutions.

4. AI Tools & Resources

Q: What are some free AI tools for beginners?
A: Google's Teachable Machine, TensorFlow, OpenAI's ChatGPT, IBM Watson, and Microsoft Azure AI.

Q: Where can I practice AI without installing software?
A: Google Colab, Kaggle Notebooks, and online AI platforms like RunwayML.

Q: Can AI help in creative fields like art and music?
A: Yes! AI is used in music composition, digital art, and even writing, through tools like DALL·E, Deep Dream, and AI-powered music generators.

---

5. Building AI Projects

Q: How do I train an AI model?
A: Training involves collecting data, preprocessing it, selecting an algorithm, training the model, and evaluating its performance.

Q: What are some beginner-friendly AI project ideas?
A: Image classification, chatbot development, sentiment analysis, and AI-based recommendations.

Q: Can I build an AI model without coding?
A: Yes, platforms like Google's Teachable Machine and AutoML allow users to create AI models without writing code.

Q: What are the ethical concerns in AI development?
A: Ethical concerns include privacy issues, job displacement, biased algorithms, and the potential misuse of AI for harmful purposes.

Q: How can I test if an AI model is reliable?
A: AI models are tested using metrics like accuracy, precision, recall, and F1 score. It's important to validate models on diverse datasets to ensure fairness and reliability.

6. Prompt Engineering in AI

Q: What is Prompt Engineering?
A: Prompt Engineering is the practice of crafting effective prompts to guide AI models like ChatGPT, Gemini, or Claude to generate the best possible responses. It involves structuring inputs strategically to get precise, relevant, and high-quality outputs.

Q: Why is Prompt Engineering important?
A: AI models respond based on the input they receive. A well-designed prompt can improve accuracy, creativity, and usefulness. It helps users get better results without needing to modify the AI model itself.

Q: How do I write a good prompt?
A: Follow these principles:

- Be clear and specific (e.g., *"Summarize this article in three bullet points."* instead of *"Summarize this."*).
- Provide context (e.g., *"Explain this concept as if you are teaching a 10-year-old."*).
- Use step-by-step instructions (e.g., *"First, define AI, then give an example, and finally explain its impact."*).

Q: What are some common prompt techniques?
A:

- **Role-based prompting:** *"Act as a data scientist and analyze this dataset."*
- **Step-by-step prompting:** *"Explain the process of machine learning in five simple steps."*
- **Few-shot prompting:** *"Here are two examples of email replies. Now generate a reply for this email."*
- **Negative prompting:** *"Explain AI, but do not use technical jargon."*

Q: Can AI remember my previous prompts?
A: Most AI chatbots do not retain memory between conversations. However, within a single chat session, they can remember context temporarily. Some advanced AI tools allow session memory for better continuity.

Q: What are some free tools to practice Prompt Engineering?
A: You can experiment with prompts on free platforms like:

- ChatGPT (OpenAI)
- Google Gemini
- Claude (Anthropic)
- Poe.com (Aggregates multiple AI models)

Q: How can I learn more about Prompt Engineering?
A: Start by experimenting with different prompt styles. OpenAI and Google provide free resources, or watch video tutorials.

7. Retrieval-Augmented Generation (RAG)

Q: What is Retrieval-Augmented Generation (RAG)?
A: RAG is a technique that combines traditional retrieval methods with generative AI models. It enhances the performance of AI by retrieving relevant information from a large corpus or database and then using that information to generate more accurate and context-aware responses. This approach is especially useful for tasks like answering complex questions, document summarization, and conversational AI.

Q: How does RAG work?
A: RAG involves two main steps:

1. **Retrieval:** The AI first searches a database or knowledge base to retrieve relevant documents or pieces of information.
2. **Generation:** The retrieved data is then fed into a generative model (e.g., GPT-4) to create a response that is both contextually relevant and informative.

Q: Why is RAG useful?

A: RAG allows AI to provide more informed and accurate answers by leveraging external knowledge, especially in cases where the model's internal knowledge is limited or outdated. This method is especially helpful for specialized topics or domains that require up-to-date information.

Q: Can RAG be used for conversational AI?

A: Yes, RAG is highly effective in building intelligent chatbots and virtual assistants. By combining retrieval from a large set of documents with generative capabilities, RAG models can engage in more natural and context-aware conversations.

Q: What are some use cases for RAG?

A: Some common use cases for RAG include:

- **Customer support:** Providing more accurate, data-driven answers based on a company's knowledge base.
- **Legal and medical research:** Answering questions with highly specific, domain-related information.
- **FAQ generation:** Automatically creating FAQs by retrieving the most relevant documents or articles.
- **Summarization:** Combining content from multiple sources into a concise summary.

Q: What tools are available to work with RAG?

A: There are several tools and frameworks available for working with RAG, including:

- **Haystack by deepset:** An open-source framework for building RAG-based pipelines.
- **LangChain:** A Python library that integrates RAG capabilities with large language models.
- **Pinecone and Weaviate:** Vector databases that support information retrieval for RAG systems.

Q: Do I need to be an expert to use RAG?

A: Not necessarily. While implementing RAG requires some technical knowledge, especially in handling databases and AI models, there are many pre-built tools and libraries (like LangChain) that simplify the process. You can start experimenting with RAG-based projects using simple tutorials.

Q: How is RAG different from traditional machine learning models?

A: Traditional models rely solely on the training data they have been exposed to, while RAG models extend this by incorporating real-time retrieval of relevant data, making them more flexible and capable of providing more accurate and contextually enriched outputs.

8. Breaking Down AI Jargon

Q: What is an AI model?

A: An AI model is a computer program that learns patterns from data and makes predictions or generates responses. It's like a trained assistant that can answer questions, recognize images, or translate languages. Some AI models are trained from **scratch** using raw data, such as custom-built neural networks for stock price prediction, medical diagnosis models, and self-trained chatbots for specific industries. Others use **pre-trained** models to speed up development.

Q: What does "pre-trained model" mean?

A: A pre-trained model is an AI that has already learned from a large dataset before being used for a specific task. Instead of starting from scratch, you can fine-tune it with new data to improve its performance for a particular job. Examples include **BERT** for NLP tasks, **VGG16** for image classification, **Whisper** for speech recognition, and **DALL·E** for image generation.

Q: What is "fine-tuning" in AI?

A: Fine-tuning is the process of taking a pre-trained AI model and training it further on a smaller, specialized dataset to improve its performance for a specific task. This allows the model to retain its general knowledge while adapting to domain-specific requirements. For example, a general chatbot like GPT can be fine-tuned on legal documents to provide more accurate answers to legal questions, or an image recognition model can be fine-tuned on medical scans to detect diseases more effectively.

Q: What is "inference" in AI?

A: Inference is the process where an AI model applies what it has learned during training to generate an output or make a decision. It happens when the model takes new input data and produces a prediction, classification, or response. For example, when you ask ChatGPT a question, it analyzes the input and generates a relevant response based on its training. Similarly, a self-driving car uses inference to recognize traffic signs and make driving decisions in real time.

Q: What is a "dataset" in AI?

A: A dataset is a structured collection of text, images, numbers, or other types of data used to train and evaluate AI models. It serves as the learning material for AI, helping it recognize patterns and make accurate predictions. High-quality datasets with diverse and well-labeled data improve model performance, while poor-quality datasets can lead to biased or inaccurate results. For example, an AI model for speech recognition may be trained on a dataset of audio recordings in multiple languages to enhance its accuracy.

Q: What does "bias in AI" mean?

A: Bias in AI happens when a model produces unfair or inaccurate results due to imbalanced or flawed training data. For example, if a hiring AI is trained mostly on resumes from one country, it may unfairly prefer applicants from that region.

Q: What is "zero-shot learning" in AI?

A: Zero-shot learning allows AI to handle tasks it hasn't seen before. For example, if a chatbot correctly answers a question on a new topic without specific training, it is using zero-shot learning.

Q: What is a "Neural Network"?

A: A neural network is a type of AI model designed to mimic the way the human brain processes information. It consists of layers of interconnected artificial "neurons" that learn patterns from data. Each neuron receives inputs, applies weights, and passes the result through an activation function to make decisions. Neural networks are widely used in deep learning for tasks like image recognition, speech processing, and language translation. Examples include **CNNs for image classification and RNNs for speech recognition.**

Q: What is "Tokenization" in AI?

A: Tokenization is the process of breaking text into smaller parts (tokens) so AI can understand it. For example, "AI is powerful" might be split into ["AI", "is", "powerful"]. AI processes these tokens instead of full sentences.

Q: What is "Generative AI"?

A: Generative AI is a type of artificial intelligence that creates new content, such as text, images, music, or code, rather than just analyzing existing data. It learns patterns from large datasets and generates outputs based on input prompts. For example, **ChatGPT** creates human-like text responses, **DALL·E** generates images from descriptions, and **MuseNet** composes music. Generative AI is used in creative writing, design, and automation to enhance productivity and innovation.

Q: What is "Hallucination" in AI?

A: AI hallucination occurs when an AI model generates false, misleading, or nonsensical information that sounds convincing but isn't true. This happens because AI models predict responses based on patterns in their training data and may "guess" when they lack accurate information. For example, a chatbot might invent a fake citation or provide incorrect historical facts. Reducing hallucinations requires high-quality training data, better fact-checking, and techniques like grounding AI responses in verified sources.

Q: What does "Overfitting" mean in AI?

A: Overfitting happens when an AI model learns patterns from training data too precisely, including noise or irrelevant details, making it perform poorly on new, unseen data. It's like a student memorizing answers instead of understanding the subject—excelling on practice tests but failing real exams. Overfitting can be reduced using techniques like **regularization, dropout, data augmentation, and cross-validation.**

Q: What is "Underfitting" in AI?

A: Underfitting occurs when an AI model fails to learn meaningful patterns from the training data, leading to poor performance on both the training set and new data. This happens when the model is too simple or lacks enough training time to capture the underlying relationships. It's like a student studying too little and struggling with both practice and real tests. Underfitting can be addressed by **using a more complex model, increasing training time, or providing more relevant features in the data.**

Q: What is "Transfer Learning"?

A: Transfer learning is when an AI model trained on one task is reused for another similar task. For example, a model trained on general images can be fine-tuned to identify medical scans.

Q: What is "Embeddings" in AI?

A: Embeddings are numerical representations of words, images, or other data that help AI models understand relationships and similarities between them. They convert complex information into dense vectors in a way that preserves meaning. For example, in a word embedding model, the word **"king"** is mapped to a vector close to **"queen"**, capturing their semantic relationship. Embeddings are widely used in **natural language processing (NLP), recommendation systems, and image recognition** to improve AI performance.

Q: What is "Vector Database"?

A: A vector database is a specialized database designed to store and search embeddings—numerical representations of data—efficiently. It enables AI models to quickly find similar images, documents, or text by comparing vectors based on their mathematical proximity. This makes it ideal for tasks like **image recognition, recommendation systems, and semantic search**. Popular vector databases include **FAISS, Pinecone, and ChromaDB.**

Q: What is "Natural Language Processing (NLP)"?

A: Natural Language Processing (NLP) is a branch of AI that enables computers to understand, interpret, and generate human language. It powers applications like **chatbots, voice assistants (e.g., Siri, Alexa), language translation (e.g., Google Translate), and sentiment analysis.** NLP combines linguistics and machine learning to help AI process text and speech in a way that feels natural to humans.

Q: What is "Supervised Learning"?

A: Supervised learning is a type of machine learning where an AI model is trained using labeled data, meaning each input has a known correct output. The model learns by mapping inputs to the correct labels and improving its predictions over time. For example, training an AI to recognize cats and dogs involves showing it images labeled as **"cat"** or **"dog"** so it can learn to classify new images accurately. Supervised learning is widely used in **image recognition, speech recognition, and spam detection.**

Q: What is "Unsupervised Learning"?

A: Unsupervised learning is a type of machine learning where an AI model discovers patterns and structures in data without labeled answers. Instead of learning from predefined categories, the model identifies hidden relationships, such as grouping similar items together. For example, in customer segmentation, AI can **cluster customers based on purchasing behavior** without being told which group they belong to. Unsupervised learning is commonly used in **anomaly detection, recommendation systems, and data compression.**

Q: What is "Reinforcement Learning"?

A: Reinforcement Learning (RL) is a type of machine learning where an AI learns by trial and error, receiving **rewards for good actions and penalties for mistakes.** Over time, it optimizes its decisions to maximize long-term rewards. RL is widely used in **robotics, game-playing AI (e.g., AlphaGo), self-driving cars, and personalized recommendations.**

Q: What is "LLM" (Large Language Model)?

A: LLM stands for **Large Language Model**, an AI trained on massive amounts of text data to understand and generate human-like language. ChatGPT and Gemini are examples of LLMs.

Q: What is "Explainability in AI"?

A: Explainability refers to how well we can understand and interpret an AI model's decisions. Some AI models are like "black boxes," making decisions without clear explanations, while others provide insights into their reasoning.

Q: What is Deep Learning?

A: Deep learning is a subset of machine learning that uses **artificial neural networks with multiple layers (deep neural networks)** to process data and learn complex patterns. It excels at tasks like **image recognition, speech processing, and natural language understanding.** Deep learning powers advanced AI applications such as **facial recognition, self-driving cars, chatbots (e.g., ChatGPT), and medical image analysis.**

Q: What is a Large Context Window in AI?

A: A large context window means an AI model can remember and process more words in a conversation or document at once. For example, a chatbot with a small window might forget earlier parts of a discussion, while one with a large window can maintain context better.

Q: What is Few-Shot Learning?

A: Few-shot learning allows AI to learn a new task with very few examples. For instance, if you show an AI just a couple of labeled images of a new object, it can recognize similar ones without extensive training.

Q: What is Multi-Modal AI?

A: Multi-modal AI can process and understand different types of data (like text, images, and audio) together. For example, ChatGPT-4 can analyze both text and images in a conversation.

Q: What is Computer Vision?

A: Computer Vision is a field of AI that helps machines interpret and analyze images and videos. It's used in applications like facial recognition, self-driving cars, and medical imaging.

Q: What is Pretraining vs. Fine-Tuning?

A: Pretraining is when an AI learns general knowledge from a massive dataset before being adapted for a specific task. Fine-tuning is the process of further training the AI on a smaller, specialized dataset to improve performance on a particular task.

Q: What is Data Augmentation in AI?

A: Data augmentation is a technique used to expand a dataset by modifying existing data. For example, in image recognition, flipping, rotating, or changing brightness in images helps AI models learn better without needing new data.

Q: What is a Loss Function in AI?

A: A loss function measures how far the AI's predictions are from the correct answers. AI models adjust their learning based on the loss function to improve accuracy.

Q: What is a Gradient Descent?

A: Gradient Descent is an optimization algorithm that helps AI models adjust their internal settings (weights) to minimize errors and improve learning over time.

Q: What is Model Drift?

A: Model drift happens when an AI model's accuracy decreases over time because the real-world data it encounters has changed from the data it was trained on. This often happens in fraud detection and recommendation systems.

Q: What is Catastrophic Forgetting in AI?

A: Catastrophic forgetting happens when an AI model trained on new data forgets what it learned from previous data. This is common in deep learning models that don't store past knowledge effectively.

Q: What is Explainable AI (XAI)?

A: Explainable AI (XAI) refers to AI systems designed to be transparent about their decisions. It helps users understand why an AI model made a particular prediction, improving trust and accountability.

Q: What is Reinforcement Learning with Human Feedback (RLHF)?

A: RLHF is a technique where AI is trained using human feedback to improve its responses. This is how models like ChatGPT are fine-tuned to be more helpful and accurate.

Q: What is Federated Learning?

A: Federated learning is a privacy-focused AI training method where data remains on users' devices instead of being sent to a central server. AI models learn from distributed data without compromising user privacy.

Q: What is a Transformer Model in AI?

A: A transformer is a deep learning model architecture designed to handle large-scale language processing tasks. Models like GPT, BERT, and T5 use transformers to understand and generate text.

Q: What is a Knowledge Graph?

A: A knowledge graph is a structured representation of information that connects concepts and relationships. Google Search and chatbots use knowledge graphs to provide relevant answers by linking related topics.

Q: What is Retrieval-Augmented Generation (RAG)?

A: RAG is an AI approach that improves responses by retrieving relevant information from an external database before generating an answer. It helps chatbots provide more accurate and up-to-date responses.

Q: What is an AI Accelerator?

A: AI accelerators, like GPUs (Graphics Processing Units) and TPUs (Tensor Processing Units), are specialized hardware designed to speed up AI computations, making training and inference faster.

Q: What is Edge AI?

A: Edge AI runs AI models directly on local devices (like smartphones and cameras) instead of relying on cloud servers. This allows for faster processing and improved privacy.

Q: What is Quantization in AI?

A: Quantization reduces the size of AI models by using lower-precision numbers, making them run faster and more efficiently, especially on edge devices.

Q: What are parameters in AI models?

Parameters are the internal variables of an AI model that are learned during training. They define how the model processes input data to make predictions. For example:

- In a neural network, parameters include weights and biases that connect neurons.
- The more parameters a model has, the more complex it can be.

When you hear about models with **billions of parameters** (e.g., GPT-3 with 175 billion parameters), it means the model has a vast number of internal variables, allowing it to capture intricate patterns in data.

Q: What is precision in Machine Learning?

Precision is a metric used to evaluate the performance of a classification model. It measures the accuracy of the positive predictions made by the model. For example:

- If a model predicts 100 emails as spam, and 90 of them are actually spam, the precision is 90%.

Formula:

$$Precision = True\ Positives/(True\ Positives + False\ Positives)$$

- **True Positives**: Correctly predicted positive cases.
- **False Positives**: Incorrectly predicted positive cases.

High precision means the model is good at avoiding false positives.

Q: What is recall in Machine Learning?

Recall (also called sensitivity) measures how well a model identifies all relevant positive cases. For example:

- If there are 100 spam emails in a dataset, and the model correctly identifies 80 of them, the recall is 80%.

Formula:

$$\text{Recall} = \text{True Positives}/(\text{True Positives} + \text{False Negatives})$$

- **True Positives**: Correctly predicted positive cases.
- **False Negatives**: Positive cases that the model missed.

High recall means the model is good at finding most of the positive cases.

Q: What is the difference between precision and recall?

- **Precision** focuses on the accuracy of positive predictions (avoiding false positives).
- **Recall** focuses on capturing as many positive cases as possible (avoiding false negatives).

For example, in a medical test:

- High **precision** means most positive test results are correct (few false alarms).
- High **recall** means most actual cases of the disease are detected (few missed cases).

Often, there's a trade-off between precision and recall, and the right balance depends on the use case.

Q: What is the F1 score?

The **F1 score** is a single metric that combines precision and recall. It is the harmonic mean of the two and is useful when you want to balance both metrics.

Formula:

$$\text{F1 Score} = 2 \times \text{Precision} \times \text{Recall}/(\text{recision} + \text{Recall})$$

The F1 score ranges from 0 to 1, where 1 is the best possible score. It is commonly used in classification tasks, especially when the dataset is imbalanced.

Q: What does "billion parameters" mean in AI models?

When an AI model has **billions of parameters**, it means the model has a very large number of internal variables that it uses to learn from data. For example:

- **GPT-3**, a language model, has 175 billion parameters.
- **PaLM**, Google's language model, has 540 billion parameters.

More parameters generally allow the model to capture more complex patterns, but they also require more computational resources and data to train.

Q: What is a confusion matrix?

A **confusion matrix** is a table used to evaluate the performance of a classification model. It shows the following:

- **True Positives (TP)**: Correctly predicted positive cases.
- **True Negatives (TN)**: Correctly predicted negative cases.

- **False Positives (FP)**: Incorrectly predicted positive cases.
- **False Negatives (FN)**: Incorrectly predicted negative cases.

The confusion matrix helps calculate metrics like precision, recall, and accuracy.

Q: What is accuracy in Machine Learning?

Accuracy measures the percentage of correct predictions made by a model.

Formula:

$$\text{Accuracy} = (\text{True Positives} + \text{True Negatives}) / \text{Total Predictions}$$

While accuracy is a useful metric, it can be misleading in imbalanced datasets (e.g., when 95% of the data belongs to one class). In such cases, precision, recall, and F1 score are more informative.

Q: What is a loss function?

A **loss function** measures how well an AI model performs by comparing its predictions to the actual values. The goal of training is to minimize the loss function. Common loss functions include:

- **Mean Squared Error (MSE)**: Used in regression tasks.
- **Cross-Entropy Loss**: Used in classification tasks.

A lower loss indicates a better-performing model.

9. Understanding AI Algorithms

Fundamental AI Algorithms

Q: What is a Neural Network?

A: A neural network is an AI model designed to mimic how the human brain processes information. It consists of layers of artificial neurons that recognize patterns and make predictions. Neural networks are widely used in deep learning applications like image recognition, natural language processing, and self-driving cars.

Q: What is Backpropagation?

A: Backpropagation is an algorithm used to train neural networks. It works by calculating the error of the model's predictions and adjusting the weights of the neurons to minimize this error over time. This process helps the model improve accuracy with each iteration.

Q: What is a Perceptron?

A: A perceptron is the simplest type of artificial neural network, consisting of a single layer of neurons. It is mainly used for binary classification tasks (e.g., determining whether an email is spam or not).

Q: What is a Decision Tree in AI?

A: A decision tree is a model that splits data into branches based on conditions, like a flowchart. It is commonly used in classification and regression tasks because it is easy to interpret and visualize.

Q: What is a Random Forest?

A: A random forest is an ensemble learning method that combines multiple decision trees to improve accuracy and reduce overfitting. It is used in various applications like fraud detection and medical diagnosis.

Q: What is a Support Vector Machine (SVM)?

A: SVM is an algorithm that finds the best boundary (hyperplane) to separate different categories in a dataset. It is widely used for text classification, image recognition, and bioinformatics.

Q: What is K-Nearest Neighbors (KNN)?

A: KNN is a simple yet powerful classification algorithm that assigns a data point to the category most common among its nearest neighbors. It is widely used in recommendation systems and handwriting recognition.

Optimization & Learning Techniques

Q: What is Gradient Descent?

A: Gradient descent is an optimization technique used to adjust a model's internal parameters to minimize errors. It helps AI models learn by gradually improving their predictions.

Q: What is Stochastic Gradient Descent (SGD)?

A: SGD is a variation of gradient descent that updates the model using a single data point at a time. This makes it computationally efficient, especially for large datasets, but also introduces more variance in updates.

Q: What is Batch Gradient Descent?

A: In batch gradient descent, the entire dataset is used to calculate the error before adjusting the model's parameters. It provides stable updates but can be computationally expensive.

Q: What is Overfitting in AI?

A: Overfitting happens when an AI model learns the training data too well, including noise, making it perform poorly on new data. This issue occurs when a model is too complex and lacks generalization.

Q: What is Regularization in Machine Learning?

A: Regularization is a technique used to prevent overfitting by adding penalties to large coefficients in the model. Common methods include **L1 regularization (Lasso)** and **L2 regularization (Ridge regression)**.

Q: What is Cross-Validation?

A: Cross-validation is a technique used to assess how well a machine learning model will perform on new, unseen data. The dataset is split into multiple parts, and training/testing are performed on different splits to ensure the model is generalizable.

Advanced AI Concepts

Q: What is Reinforcement Learning?

A: Reinforcement learning is an AI approach where models learn by trial and error, receiving rewards for good actions and penalties for bad ones. It is used in robotics, gaming, and autonomous systems.

Q: What is an Evolutionary Algorithm?

A: Evolutionary algorithms are inspired by natural selection and genetic evolution. They improve models over multiple generations by selecting the best-performing solutions and introducing mutations to explore new possibilities.

Q: What is the Monte Carlo Method?

A: The Monte Carlo method is a probabilistic algorithm that uses random sampling to solve complex problems. It is used in AI for decision-making, reinforcement learning, and risk analysis.

Q: What is a Genetic Algorithm?

A: A genetic algorithm is an optimization method that mimics biological evolution. It creates multiple solutions, selects the best ones, and combines them to evolve better solutions over time.

Q: What is Bayesian Optimization?

A: Bayesian optimization is a technique used for optimizing expensive functions. It is commonly used in hyperparameter tuning of machine learning models.

Q: What is Principal Component Analysis (PCA)?

A: PCA is a dimensionality reduction technique that helps in reducing the number of input variables while preserving important information. It is useful in high-dimensional datasets like image processing and bioinformatics.

Q: What is Clustering in Machine Learning?

A: Clustering is an unsupervised learning technique that groups similar data points together. Common clustering algorithms include **K-Means, DBSCAN, and Hierarchical Clustering**.

Deep Learning & Transformer Models

Q: What is a Transformer Model?

A: A transformer model is a type of deep learning model that processes input data all at once, rather than sequentially. This allows it to handle long-range dependencies efficiently, making it ideal for tasks like text generation and translation (e.g., ChatGPT, BERT).

Q: What is an Autoencoder?

A: An autoencoder is a neural network designed to compress and then reconstruct data. It is commonly used for image compression, anomaly detection, and data denoising.

Q: What is a Convolutional Neural Network (CNN)?

A: CNNs are specialized neural networks designed for image processing tasks. They use convolutional layers to detect patterns such as edges, textures, and objects in images.

Q: What is a Recurrent Neural Network (RNN)?

A: RNNs are designed for sequential data processing, such as time series prediction, speech recognition, and natural language processing. Unlike regular neural networks, RNNs can maintain memory of previous inputs.

Q: What is a Long Short-Term Memory (LSTM) Network?

A: LSTM is an advanced form of RNN that can remember long-term dependencies, making it effective for speech recognition and text generation.

Q: What is an Attention Mechanism in AI?

A: Attention is a mechanism that helps models focus on the most important parts of input data. It improves performance in tasks like language translation, image captioning, and question-answering.

10. Python's Role in AI Development

Why is Python the preferred language for AI development?

Python is the most widely used programming language in AI development due to its **simplicity, readability, and vast ecosystem of libraries**. Its syntax is intuitive, making it easy for both beginners and experienced developers to prototype and build AI applications efficiently. Additionally, Python offers **cross-platform compatibility** and has a massive community that continuously improves AI-related tools and frameworks.

What are the key Python libraries used in AI?

Python provides several powerful libraries and frameworks tailored for AI and machine learning:

- **NumPy & Pandas** – Essential for numerical computations and data manipulation.
- **Scikit-learn** – A widely used library for classical machine learning algorithms, such as decision trees, SVMs, and random forests.
- **TensorFlow & PyTorch** – The two dominant deep learning frameworks used for neural networks and large-scale AI models.
- **NLTK & SpaCy** – Libraries for natural language processing (NLP), including text parsing, sentiment analysis, and named entity recognition.
- **OpenCV** – A powerful tool for computer vision tasks, including image processing, face recognition, and object detection.
- **LangChain** – Used for building conversational AI, Retrieval-Augmented Generation (RAG), and chatbot applications.
- **Dask & PySpark** – Tools for handling big data and parallel computing in AI applications.

Can Python be used for real-time AI applications?

Yes! Python supports real-time AI applications such as **speech recognition, fraud detection, and AI-powered trading systems**. However, Python's performance limitations require optimizations for real-time processing. Techniques like **multi-threading, parallel processing, GPU acceleration (CUDA), and using Cython or Numba** can significantly improve speed. Fast frameworks like **FastAPI** are also used for deploying real-time AI models via web services.

How does Python support deep learning?

Deep learning has become a key area of AI, and Python plays a crucial role in its development. Libraries like **TensorFlow, PyTorch, and Keras** simplify the creation of complex neural networks. These frameworks provide **pre-trained models, GPU/TPU acceleration, and automatic differentiation tools**, making deep learning more accessible to developers.

Python-based deep learning models are used in tasks like **image classification, speech recognition, autonomous driving, and AI-based drug discovery**.

Is Python fast enough for AI?

While Python is not as fast as compiled languages like C++ or Java, it compensates with **optimized AI libraries** that rely on low-level implementations for performance-critical tasks. Python's integration with **C, C++, and CUDA** allows it to leverage hardware acceleration for demanding AI computations. Additionally, using **vectorized operations, multiprocessing, and distributed computing** helps Python handle large-scale AI tasks efficiently.

How does Python integrate with big data for AI?

Python is widely used in big data applications because it integrates seamlessly with frameworks like **Apache Spark (PySpark), Dask, and Hadoop**. These tools enable AI models to process **massive datasets** efficiently through **distributed computing, in-memory processing, and real-time analytics**. Python's capability to handle structured and unstructured data makes it ideal for AI-driven data science applications.

Can Python be used for AI in edge devices (IoT, mobile, etc.)?

Yes! AI models built with Python can be optimized and deployed on edge devices, such as **Raspberry Pi, mobile phones, smart cameras, and IoT sensors**. Frameworks like **TensorFlow Lite, ONNX, and TinyML** allow AI models to run on low-power hardware while maintaining efficiency. Python is widely used in **AI-powered home automation, smart surveillance, and AI-driven robotics**.

How is Python used in AI chatbots?

Python is the backbone of modern AI chatbots. Libraries like **LangChain, GPT-4 API, Rasa, and Transformers** enable developers to create **context-aware, intelligent virtual assistants**. Python-powered chatbots are used in:

- **Customer service** (e.g., AI support agents)
- **Healthcare** (e.g., AI-powered medical assistants)
- **E-commerce** (e.g., AI shopping assistants)
- **Education** (e.g., AI tutors and virtual learning assistants)

Python's ability to handle **natural language processing (NLP), sentiment analysis, and contextual memory** makes it an excellent choice for chatbot development.

What are some real-world AI applications built using Python?

Python is behind many cutting-edge AI applications, including:

- **Self-driving cars** – Tesla's AI models for autonomous driving are built using Python-powered deep learning frameworks.
- **Healthcare diagnostics** – AI models using Python detect diseases like cancer and diabetic retinopathy from medical images.
- **Fraud detection** – Financial institutions use Python-based AI systems to identify fraudulent transactions in real-time.
- **AI-powered chatbots** – Chatbots like ChatGPT, Google Assistant, and Alexa are trained using Python's NLP libraries.
- **Recommendation systems** – Streaming services like Netflix and e-commerce platforms like Amazon use Python-based AI to personalize recommendations.
- **Stock market prediction** – AI models built in Python analyze market trends and predict stock price movements.

How can I start learning Python for AI development?

To get started with Python for AI, follow these steps:

1. **Learn Python basics** – Understand variables, loops, functions, and object-oriented programming.
2. **Master data handling** – Explore **NumPy and Pandas** for data manipulation.
3. **Study machine learning** – Learn **Scikit-learn** to build predictive models.
4. **Explore deep learning** – Experiment with **TensorFlow or PyTorch** to create neural networks.
5. **Work on real-world projects** – Start building AI applications like **chatbots, image recognition systems, and NLP-based tools**.
6. **Stay updated** – Follow AI research papers, blogs, and open-source projects to keep up with advancements in the field.

Python's dominance in AI development ensures that learning it opens doors to a vast range of career opportunities in AI, machine learning, and data science.

11. Relationship Between AI and Data Science

1. How are AI and Data Science related?

AI (Artificial Intelligence) and Data Science are closely related fields but serve different purposes. **Data Science** focuses on extracting insights from data through analysis, visualization, and statistical modeling. **AI**, on the other hand, aims to create intelligent systems that can learn, reason, and make decisions autonomously. Data Science provides the foundation for AI by cleaning, organizing, and preparing data, which AI models use for training and prediction. While Data Science often uses AI techniques like Machine Learning, AI relies on Data Science to ensure the quality and relevance of its input data.

2. Why is Data Science important for AI?

Data Science plays a critical role in AI development. AI models require large volumes of structured and unstructured data to identify patterns and generate accurate predictions. Without proper data preprocessing, feature engineering, and statistical analysis, AI models may perform poorly or produce biased results. Data Science ensures that the data fed into AI systems is clean, relevant, and optimized for learning.

---

3. How does Machine Learning fit into AI and Data Science?

Machine Learning (ML) is a subset of AI that enables machines to learn from data without explicit programming. It is also a key tool in Data Science, where it is used to uncover patterns, make predictions, and automate decision-making. Here's how they fit together:

- **AI**: A broad field that includes ML, deep learning, and expert systems.
- **ML**: A subset of AI that focuses on algorithms for learning from data.
- **Data Science**: A multidisciplinary field that uses statistics, ML, and data analysis to derive insights.

Deep Learning, a more advanced subset of ML, is often used for complex tasks like image recognition and natural language processing.

---

4. What are the key differences between AI and Data Science?

Here's a quick comparison:

Feature	AI	Data Science
Definition	Builds intelligent systems that simulate human cognition.	Extracts insights from data using analytics and ML.
Goal	Develop self-learning models for automation and decision-making.	Analyze, visualize, and interpret data for business insights.
Key Techniques	Machine Learning, Deep Learning, NLP, Computer Vision.	Data Wrangling, Exploratory Data Analysis, Statistical Modeling.

Outcome	AI-powered solutions (e.g., chatbots, recommendation engines).	Data-driven decisions, predictive analytics, and business intelligence.
Tools	TensorFlow, PyTorch, OpenCV, GPT models.	Pandas, NumPy, Scikit-learn, Matplotlib, Power BI.

5. How dependent is AI on Data Science?

AI relies heavily on data, and Data Science ensures that this data is usable. While AI can technically work with raw data, it is highly inefficient without preprocessing. Data Science improves the efficiency and accuracy of AI models by cleaning, organizing, and selecting relevant features. In essence, Data Science acts as the backbone of AI development.

6. Which field has more career opportunities: AI or Data Science?

Both AI and Data Science are in high demand, but the choice depends on your interests:
- If you enjoy coding, algorithm design, and automation, consider **AI and Machine Learning roles** (e.g., AI Engineer, Deep Learning Engineer).
- If you prefer working with data, statistics, and insights, explore **Data Science roles** (e.g., Data Scientist, Data Analyst, BI Analyst).

Many roles overlap, and professionals often transition between the two fields as they gain experience.

7. Do Data Scientists need to learn AI?

While not mandatory, learning AI can significantly enhance a Data Scientist's skill set. Many modern Data Science applications use Machine Learning and AI to improve predictions and automate decision-making. Familiarity with AI techniques like Neural Networks, NLP, and Computer Vision can help Data Scientists tackle more complex problems and stay competitive in the job market.

8. Is Python used in both AI and Data Science?

Yes, Python is the dominant language for both fields due to its extensive ecosystem of libraries:
- **For Data Science**: Pandas, NumPy, Scikit-learn, Matplotlib, Seaborn.
- **For AI & Machine Learning**: TensorFlow, PyTorch, OpenCV, LangChain, Hugging Face Transformers.

Python's simplicity, flexibility, and powerful libraries make it the preferred choice for data processing, model training, and AI development.

9. What industries use AI and Data Science?

AI and Data Science are transforming industries across the board:
- **Healthcare**: AI-driven diagnostics, personalized medicine, predictive analytics.
- **Finance**: Fraud detection, risk assessment, AI-powered trading.
- **E-commerce**: Recommendation systems, customer behavior analysis.
- **Manufacturing**: Predictive maintenance, quality control automation.
- **Automotive**: Self-driving technology, AI-assisted navigation.
- **Entertainment**: Content recommendation, AI-generated media.
- **Climate Science**: AI for climate modeling and environmental monitoring.

10. Which field should I learn first: Data Science or AI?

It depends on your career goals:
- If you want to start with fundamentals, learn **Data Science** first. It covers data manipulation, visualization, and basic ML algorithms.
- If you're interested in AI applications like chatbots, computer vision, and deep learning, start with **Machine Learning and AI**.

A balanced approach is to begin with Data Science basics and gradually move into AI and ML. Foundational skills in mathematics (linear algebra, calculus) and programming (Python, R) are essential for both fields.

11. What are the ethical considerations in AI and Data Science?

Both fields raise important ethical questions, such as:
- **Bias in AI Models**: Poorly trained models can perpetuate biases present in the data.
- **Data Privacy**: Handling sensitive data requires strict compliance with regulations like GDPR.
- **Transparency**: Ensuring AI systems are explainable and their decisions are understandable.

Ethical practices are critical to building trust and ensuring the responsible use of AI and Data Science.

12. What are the emerging trends in AI and Data Science?

The fields are evolving rapidly, with trends like:
- **Generative AI**: Tools like GPT and DALL·E for creating text, images, and more.
- **Edge Computing**: Running AI models on local devices for faster processing.
- **Federated Learning**: Training models across decentralized devices while preserving privacy.
- **AI for Sustainability**: Using AI to address climate change and environmental challenges.

12. Common Myths and Misconceptions About AI

Artificial Intelligence (AI) is one of the most exciting and rapidly evolving fields today. However, it is also surrounded by myths and misconceptions that can lead to confusion or unrealistic expectations. Let's debunk some of the most common myths about AI.

---

1. Is AI the same as human intelligence?

No, AI is not the same as human intelligence. While AI can mimic certain aspects of human cognition, such as learning and problem-solving, it lacks consciousness, emotions, and true understanding. AI systems are designed to perform specific tasks based on data and algorithms, but they do not possess general intelligence or self-awareness.

---

2. Can AI work without data?

No, AI cannot work without data. Data is the foundation of AI, as it is used to train models, identify patterns, and make predictions. Without high-quality, relevant data, AI systems cannot function effectively. This is why Data Science, which focuses on collecting, cleaning, and analyzing data, is so critical to AI development.

---

3. Is AI only for large tech companies?

No, AI is not limited to large tech companies. While companies like Google, Microsoft, and Amazon have been pioneers in AI, the technology is becoming increasingly accessible to smaller businesses, startups, and even individuals. Open-source tools, cloud-based AI services, and affordable hardware have democratized AI, enabling anyone with the right skills to build AI solutions.

---

4. Will AI eventually take over the world?

No, AI will not take over the world. This is a common misconception fueled by science fiction. AI is a tool created and controlled by humans, and its capabilities are limited to the tasks it is designed for. While AI can automate certain processes and make decisions based on data, it does not have intentions, desires, or the ability to act independently.

---

5. Can AI solve all problems?

No, AI cannot solve all problems. While AI is incredibly powerful, it is not a magic solution. AI is best suited for tasks that involve pattern recognition, data analysis, and automation. It struggles with tasks that require creativity, empathy, or deep contextual understanding. Additionally, AI systems are only as good as the data they are trained on, and poor-quality data can lead to inaccurate or biased results.

---

6. Is AI unbiased and fair?

No, AI is not inherently unbiased or fair. AI systems learn from data, and if the data contains biases, the AI model will likely replicate or even amplify those biases. For example, biased hiring algorithms can discriminate against certain groups if the training data reflects historical inequalities. Ensuring fairness in AI requires careful data selection, preprocessing, and ongoing monitoring.

---

7. Does AI always outperform humans?

No, AI does not always outperform humans. While AI excels at tasks like data processing, pattern recognition, and repetitive tasks, it often falls short in areas that require creativity, intuition, and emotional intelligence. For example, AI can generate art or music, but it lacks the depth of meaning and emotional resonance that human creators bring to their work.

---

8. Is AI too complex for beginners to learn?

No, AI is not too complex for beginners to learn. While AI involves advanced concepts like machine learning, neural networks, and algorithms, there are many beginner-friendly resources, tools, and frameworks available. Platforms like TensorFlow, Scikit-learn, and Fast.ai offer tutorials and documentation to help newcomers get started. With dedication and practice, anyone can learn the basics of AI.

---

9. Will AI replace all human jobs?

No, AI will not replace all human jobs. While AI can automate certain tasks, it is more likely to augment human capabilities rather than replace them entirely. Many jobs require skills like creativity, critical thinking, and emotional intelligence, which AI cannot replicate. Instead of eliminating jobs, AI is expected to create new roles and opportunities in fields like AI development, data science, and AI ethics.

---

10. Is AI only about robots and automation?

No, AI is not just about robots and automation. While robotics is one application of AI, the field is much broader. AI includes technologies like natural language processing (e.g., chatbots), computer vision (e.g., facial recognition), recommendation systems (e.g., Netflix recommendations), and more. AI is also used in healthcare, finance, education, and many other industries.

---

11. Can AI think for itself?

No, AI cannot think for itself. AI systems operate based on predefined algorithms and data. They do not have consciousness, self-awareness, or the ability to make independent decisions. Even advanced AI models like GPT or deep learning systems are simply following patterns and rules learned from data, not "thinking" in the way humans do.

---

12. Is AI only for tech-savvy people?

No, AI is not only for tech-savvy people. While a technical background can be helpful, many AI tools and platforms are designed to be user-friendly. For example, no-code AI platforms allow non-technical users to build AI models using drag-and-drop interfaces. Additionally, understanding the basics of AI does not require advanced programming skills—just curiosity and a willingness to learn.

---

13. Is AI always expensive to develop?

No, AI development is not always expensive. While building advanced AI systems can require significant resources, there are many affordable and even free tools available for beginners. Open-source libraries like TensorFlow and PyTorch, along with cloud-based AI services, have made it easier and more cost-effective to experiment with AI.

---

14. Is AI a recent invention?

No, AI is not a recent invention. The concept of AI has been around since the 1950s, and early AI research laid the groundwork for many of the technologies we use today. What has changed in recent years is the availability of massive amounts of data, powerful computing resources, and advanced algorithms, which have accelerated AI development and adoption.

---

15. Is AI only about machine learning?

No, AI is not only about machine learning (ML). While ML is a major subset of AI, the field also includes other techniques like rule-based systems, expert systems, and evolutionary algorithms. AI encompasses a wide range of technologies and approaches aimed at creating intelligent systems.

13. **AI and the Law**

As Artificial Intelligence (AI) becomes more integrated into our lives, it raises important legal and regulatory questions. From intellectual property to liability, AI is challenging traditional legal frameworks. Here are some common questions about AI and the law:

---

1. What are the legal implications of AI decision-making?

AI systems are increasingly used to make decisions in areas like hiring, lending, and law enforcement. However, these decisions can have significant consequences, and questions arise about accountability. For example:
- Who is responsible if an AI system makes a biased or incorrect decision?
- Can AI decisions be challenged in court?

- How can we ensure transparency and fairness in AI decision-making?

These questions highlight the need for clear legal frameworks to govern the use of AI in decision-making processes.

---

2. How is AI regulated in different countries?

AI regulation varies widely across the globe. Some countries, like the European Union, have taken a proactive approach with initiatives like the **AI Act**, which aims to ensure AI systems are safe, transparent, and ethical. In contrast, other countries have more relaxed regulations, focusing on innovation and economic growth. Key areas of regulation include:
- Data privacy and protection (e.g., GDPR in the EU).
- Bias and discrimination in AI systems.
- Safety and reliability of AI technologies.

As AI continues to evolve, international collaboration will be essential to create consistent and effective regulations.

---

3. What are the challenges of intellectual property (IP) in AI-generated content?

AI is increasingly used to create art, music, literature, and even inventions. This raises complex questions about intellectual property:
- Who owns the rights to AI-generated content—the developer, the user, or the AI itself?
- Can AI-generated works be copyrighted or patented?
- What happens if an AI system replicates someone else's work without permission?

These challenges are forcing legal systems to adapt and rethink traditional IP laws.

---

4. Can AI be used in legal research and practice?

Yes, AI is already transforming the legal profession. Tools like **natural language processing (NLP)** are being used to:
- Analyze legal documents and contracts.
- Predict case outcomes based on historical data.
- Automate routine tasks like document review and legal research.

While AI can improve efficiency and reduce costs, it also raises concerns about job displacement and the need for legal professionals to adapt to new technologies.

---

5. What are the liability issues with AI?

Liability is a major concern when AI systems cause harm or make mistakes. For example:
- If a self-driving car causes an accident, who is liable—the manufacturer, the software developer, or the user?
- If an AI-powered medical device fails, who is responsible—the doctor, the hospital, or the tech company?

These questions are still being debated, and legal systems are working to establish clear guidelines for AI-related liability.

6. How does AI impact data privacy and security?

AI systems rely on vast amounts of data, which often includes sensitive personal information. This raises important privacy and security concerns:

- How can we ensure that AI systems comply with data protection laws like GDPR?
- What safeguards are needed to prevent data breaches and misuse of personal information?
- Can AI itself be used to enhance data security, such as detecting cyber threats?

Balancing the benefits of AI with the need to protect privacy is a key challenge for lawmakers.

7. Can AI be used to enforce laws?

Yes, AI is being used in law enforcement for tasks like:

- Predictive policing to identify potential crime hotspots.
- Facial recognition to identify suspects.
- Analyzing evidence and detecting patterns in criminal activity.

However, these applications raise ethical and legal concerns, such as the risk of bias, discrimination, and violations of civil liberties.

8. What are the ethical considerations in AI and the law?

AI poses several ethical challenges for the legal system, including:

- Ensuring fairness and avoiding bias in AI systems.
- Protecting individual rights and freedoms in the age of AI surveillance.
- Promoting transparency and accountability in AI decision-making.

Ethical guidelines and legal frameworks are essential to ensure that AI is used responsibly and for the benefit of society.

9. How can AI help improve access to justice?

AI has the potential to make legal services more accessible and affordable. For example:

- Chatbots can provide basic legal advice and information.
- Online platforms can connect people with affordable legal services.
- AI tools can help individuals navigate complex legal systems.

However, it is important to ensure that these technologies do not exclude vulnerable populations or compromise the quality of legal services.

10. What is the future of AI and the law?

The future of AI and the law will likely involve:

- New regulations to address emerging challenges like deepfakes, autonomous weapons, and AI-generated content.
- Greater collaboration between technologists, legal experts, and policymakers.

- Ongoing debates about the balance between innovation and regulation.

As AI continues to evolve, the legal system must adapt to ensure that it remains fair, transparent, and accountable.

14. AI and Creativity

Artificial Intelligence (AI) is not just about numbers and algorithms—it's also making waves in the world of creativity. From generating art and music to assisting writers and designers, AI is transforming how we think about creativity. Here are some common questions about AI and its role in creative fields:

---

1. Can AI be creative?

Yes, AI can exhibit creativity, but it's different from human creativity. AI systems can generate art, music, and text by learning patterns from existing data. However, AI lacks consciousness, emotions, and the ability to experience the world, which are key aspects of human creativity. Instead, AI's "creativity" is based on combining and reinterpreting existing ideas in novel ways.

---

2. How is AI used in art?

AI is being used in art in various ways:
- **Generative Art**: AI tools like DeepArt and DALL·E create original artwork based on user inputs or styles learned from existing art.
- **Style Transfer**: AI can apply the style of one artwork (e.g., Van Gogh's brushstrokes) to another image.
- **Collaboration**: Artists are using AI as a tool to enhance their creative process, experimenting with new forms of expression.

While AI-generated art is impressive, it often raises questions about authorship and originality.

---

3. Can AI compose music?

Yes, AI can compose music. Tools like OpenAI's MuseNet and Google's Magenta use machine learning to generate melodies, harmonies, and even entire compositions. AI can also:
- Mimic the style of famous composers.
- Create background music for videos and games.
- Assist musicians by suggesting chord progressions or melodies.

However, AI-generated music often lacks the emotional depth and storytelling that human composers bring to their work.

---

4. How is AI used in writing?

AI is transforming the writing process in several ways:
- **Content Generation**: Tools like GPT-3 can write articles, stories, and even poetry based on prompts.

- **Editing and Proofreading**: AI tools like Grammarly help writers improve grammar, style, and clarity.
- **Idea Generation**: AI can suggest topics, headlines, or plot ideas to inspire writers.

While AI can assist with writing, it still struggles with creating truly original or emotionally resonant content.

---

5. Can AI replace human creators?

No, AI is unlikely to replace human creators entirely. While AI can generate impressive content, it lacks the ability to:
- Understand complex human emotions and experiences.
- Create works with deep meaning or cultural significance.
- Innovate in ways that challenge societal norms or push boundaries.

Instead, AI is best seen as a tool that can augment and enhance human creativity, not replace it.

---

6. What are the limitations of AI in creative tasks?

AI has several limitations in creative fields:
- **Lack of Originality**: AI relies on existing data and patterns, so its creations are often derivative.
- **Emotional Depth**: AI cannot truly understand or convey emotions, which are central to many creative works.
- **Contextual Understanding**: AI struggles with nuanced cultural, historical, or social contexts that inform human creativity.

These limitations mean that AI is better suited to assisting creators rather than replacing them.

---

7. How can humans and AI collaborate in creative processes?

AI can be a powerful collaborator for human creators:
- **Inspiration**: AI can generate ideas, styles, or concepts that creators can build upon.
- **Efficiency**: AI can handle repetitive or time-consuming tasks, allowing creators to focus on higher-level work.
- **Experimentation**: AI enables creators to explore new techniques and styles that might be difficult or time-consuming to achieve manually.

For example, a musician might use AI to generate a melody and then refine it to add emotional depth and personal expression.

---

8. What are some examples of AI in creative industries?

AI is being used in various creative industries:
- **Film and Animation**: AI tools can generate special effects, animate characters, and even write scripts.
- **Fashion**: AI helps designers predict trends, create patterns, and personalize clothing designs.

- **Gaming**: AI is used to create realistic environments, design characters, and generate dynamic storylines.
- **Advertising**: AI generates ad copy, designs visuals, and optimizes campaigns for target audiences.

These applications demonstrate the versatility of AI in enhancing creativity across industries.

---

9. What are the ethical concerns around AI and creativity?

AI in creativity raises several ethical questions:
- **Authorship**: Who owns the rights to AI-generated content—the developer, the user, or the AI itself?
- **Bias**: AI systems can perpetuate biases present in the data they are trained on, leading to unfair or harmful outcomes.
- **Authenticity**: How do we ensure that AI-generated works are not misrepresented as human-created?

Addressing these concerns requires clear guidelines and ethical frameworks for the use of AI in creative fields.

---

10. What is the future of AI and creativity?

The future of AI and creativity is full of possibilities:
- **Enhanced Collaboration**: AI will continue to serve as a tool for creators, enabling new forms of expression and innovation.
- **Personalization**: AI will allow for more personalized creative experiences, such as custom music playlists or tailored art recommendations.
- **New Art Forms**: AI will inspire entirely new genres of art, music, and literature that blend human and machine creativity.

As AI evolves, it will open up exciting opportunities for creators to push the boundaries of what's possible.

15. AI and Robotics

Artificial Intelligence (AI) and robotics are two fields that often go hand in hand. While robotics focuses on building physical machines, AI provides the "brain" that enables these machines to perform tasks autonomously. Together, they are transforming industries and creating new possibilities. Here are some common questions about AI and robotics:

---

1. What is the role of AI in robotics?

AI is the intelligence that powers robots, enabling them to:
- **Perceive Their Environment**: Using sensors, cameras, and microphones, robots can gather data about their surroundings.
- **Make Decisions**: AI algorithms process the data and help robots decide how to act.

- **Learn and Adapt**: Machine Learning allows robots to improve their performance over time based on experience.

Without AI, robots would be limited to pre-programmed tasks and unable to handle complex or unpredictable situations.

---

2. How are AI-powered robots being used in industries?

AI-powered robots are revolutionizing various industries:
- **Manufacturing**: Robots assemble products, perform quality checks, and handle hazardous materials.
- **Healthcare**: Surgical robots assist doctors with precision surgeries, while robotic exoskeletons help patients with mobility issues.
- **Agriculture**: Robots plant seeds, monitor crops, and harvest produce autonomously.
- **Logistics**: Warehouse robots sort, pack, and transport goods efficiently.
- **Retail**: Robots assist customers, manage inventory, and even clean stores.

These applications demonstrate how AI and robotics are improving efficiency, safety, and productivity.

---

3. What are the challenges of integrating AI into robotics?

Integrating AI into robotics comes with several challenges:
- **Complexity**: Developing AI algorithms that can handle real-world variability is difficult.
- **Cost**: Advanced AI-powered robots can be expensive to develop and maintain.
- **Safety**: Ensuring that robots operate safely around humans is a major concern.
- **Ethics**: Addressing concerns about job displacement and the ethical use of AI in robotics.

Overcoming these challenges requires collaboration between engineers, researchers, and policymakers.

---

4. Can AI-powered robots learn on their own?

Yes, AI-powered robots can learn on their own using techniques like **Reinforcement Learning** and **Unsupervised Learning**. For example:
- A robot can learn to navigate a maze by trial and error, improving its path over time.
- A robotic arm can learn to pick up objects of different shapes and sizes by practicing.

However, this learning process requires significant computational resources and data.

---

5. What are some examples of AI-powered robots?

Here are a few notable examples of AI-powered robots:
- **Self-Driving Cars**: Use AI to perceive their environment, make driving decisions, and navigate safely.
- **Sophia**: A humanoid robot developed by Hanson Robotics that can hold conversations and express emotions.

- **Boston Dynamics' Robots**: Like Spot and Atlas, which can walk, run, and perform complex tasks.
- **Da Vinci Surgical System**: A robotic system that assists surgeons with minimally invasive procedures.

These examples highlight the diverse applications of AI in robotics.

---

6. How do robots use AI to interact with humans?

AI enables robots to interact with humans in natural and intuitive ways:

- **Natural Language Processing (NLP)**: Allows robots to understand and respond to spoken or written language.
- **Computer Vision**: Helps robots recognize faces, gestures, and emotions.
- **Speech Synthesis**: Enables robots to speak and communicate effectively.

These capabilities make robots more user-friendly and accessible.

---

7. What is the future of AI and robotics?

The future of AI and robotics is full of exciting possibilities:

- **Collaborative Robots (Cobots)**: Robots that work alongside humans in shared spaces, enhancing productivity and safety.
- **Personal Robots**: Robots that assist with household tasks, care for the elderly, or provide companionship.
- **Autonomous Systems**: Self-driving vehicles, drones, and delivery robots that operate without human intervention.
- **AI-Driven Innovation**: New applications in fields like space exploration, disaster response, and environmental monitoring.

As AI and robotics continue to advance, they will play an increasingly important role in our daily lives.

---

8. What are the ethical concerns around AI and robotics?

AI-powered robotics raises several ethical questions:

- **Job Displacement**: How can we ensure that automation does not lead to widespread unemployment?
- **Privacy**: How do we protect personal data collected by robots?
- **Safety**: How can we ensure that robots operate safely and reliably?
- **Bias**: How do we prevent AI algorithms from perpetuating biases in robotic systems?

Addressing these concerns requires careful planning, regulation, and ethical guidelines.

---

9. Can I build my own AI-powered robot?

Yes, you can build your own AI-powered robot! Here's how to get started:

- **Learn the Basics**: Study robotics, electronics, and programming (Python and C++ are commonly used).

- **Use Development Kits**: Platforms like Arduino and Raspberry Pi are great for beginners.
- **Experiment with AI**: Integrate AI libraries like TensorFlow or OpenCV to add intelligence to your robot.
- **Join Communities**: Participate in robotics forums, hackathons, and maker spaces to learn from others.

Building a robot is a fun and rewarding way to apply your AI and robotics knowledge.

---

10. What skills are needed to work in AI and robotics?

Working in AI and robotics requires a mix of technical and creative skills:
- **Programming**: Proficiency in languages like Python, C++, or Java.
- **Mathematics**: Strong understanding of linear algebra, calculus, and probability.
- **Electronics**: Knowledge of circuits, sensors, and microcontrollers.
- **Problem-Solving**: Ability to design and troubleshoot complex systems.
- **Creativity**: Thinking outside the box to develop innovative solutions.

With these skills, you can pursue careers in robotics engineering, AI research, or automation.

AI and robotics are transforming the way we live and work, from manufacturing and healthcare to entertainment and beyond. By combining the physical capabilities of robots with the intelligence of AI, we can create systems that are smarter, more efficient, and more adaptable than ever before. Whether you're a beginner or an experienced professional, the world of AI and robotics offers endless opportunities to learn, innovate, and make a difference.

16. Getting Started with AI: A Step-by-Step Guide

Artificial Intelligence (AI) can seem intimidating at first, but with the right approach, anyone can start learning and experimenting with AI. Whether you're a complete beginner or someone with a bit of technical background, this step-by-step guide will help you get started on your AI journey.

---

1. What are the first steps to learning AI?

Starting with AI doesn't have to be overwhelming. Here's how to begin:
- **Understand the Basics**: Learn what AI is, its applications, and its key concepts (e.g., Machine Learning, Deep Learning).
- **Set Clear Goals**: Decide why you want to learn AI—whether it's for a career, a project, or personal interest.
- **Learn the Prerequisites**: Build a foundation in mathematics (linear algebra, calculus, probability) and programming (Python is highly recommended).

---

2. What resources are best for beginners?

There are plenty of beginner-friendly resources to help you learn AI:

- **Online Courses**: Platforms like Coursera, edX, and Udacity offer introductory AI courses.
- **YouTube Channels**: Channels like *3Blue1Brown* (for math) and *Sentdex* (for Python and AI) are great for visual learners.
- **Interactive Platforms**: Websites like Kaggle and DataCamp offer hands-on tutorials and projects.

---

3. What programming language should I learn for AI?

Python is the most popular language for AI and Machine Learning because of its simplicity and extensive libraries. Here's how to get started:
- Learn Python basics (variables, loops, functions).
- Explore Python libraries for AI, such as:
  - **NumPy** and **Pandas** for data manipulation.
  - **Matplotlib** and **Seaborn** for data visualization.
  - **Scikit-learn** for Machine Learning.
  - **TensorFlow** and **PyTorch** for Deep Learning.

---

4. How can I practice AI skills?

Practice is key to mastering AI. Here are some ways to get hands-on experience:
- **Work on Projects**: Start with simple projects like predicting house prices or classifying images.
- **Participate in Competitions**: Platforms like Kaggle host AI competitions where you can solve real-world problems.
- **Build a Portfolio**: Showcase your projects on GitHub or a personal website to demonstrate your skills to potential employers.

---

5. What are some beginner-friendly AI projects?

Here are a few beginner-friendly AI projects to get you started:
- **Predictive Analytics**: Predict stock prices or weather using regression models.
- **Image Classification**: Build a model to classify images of cats and dogs.
- **Chatbot**: Create a simple chatbot using Natural Language Processing (NLP).
- **Recommendation System**: Build a movie or product recommendation system.

These projects will help you apply what you've learned and build confidence in your skills.

---

6. Do I need a powerful computer to learn AI?

Not necessarily. While advanced AI models (e.g., deep learning) require significant computational power, you can start with:

- **Cloud Platforms**: Use cloud services like Google Colab, AWS, or Microsoft Azure to run AI models without needing a high-end computer.
- **Pre-trained Models**: Use pre-trained models available in libraries like TensorFlow Hub or Hugging Face to avoid training models from scratch.

As you progress, you can invest in better hardware or continue using cloud resources.

---

7. How can I stay updated on AI trends?

AI is a fast-evolving field, so staying updated is crucial. Here's how:
- **Follow AI News**: Websites like *Towards Data Science*, *AI News*, and *MIT Technology Review* provide the latest updates.
- **Join Communities**: Participate in AI forums like Reddit's r/MachineLearning or LinkedIn groups.
- **Attend Events**: Join webinars, conferences, and meetups to network with professionals and learn about new developments.

---

8. Should I specialize in a specific area of AI?

As you progress, you may want to specialize in areas like:
- **Machine Learning**: Focus on algorithms and models for prediction and classification.
- **Deep Learning**: Dive into neural networks for tasks like image and speech recognition.
- **Natural Language Processing (NLP)**: Work on language-related applications like chatbots and translation.
- **Computer Vision**: Explore AI for image and video analysis.

Specializing can help you build expertise and stand out in the job market.

---

9. How long does it take to learn AI?

The time it takes to learn AI depends on your background and goals:
- **Beginners**: With consistent effort, you can learn the basics in 3-6 months.
- **Intermediate Learners**: Building practical skills and completing projects may take 6-12 months.
- **Advanced Learners**: Mastering advanced topics and specializing can take 1-2 years or more.

Remember, learning AI is a continuous process, and staying curious is key.

---

10. What are the career opportunities in AI?

AI offers a wide range of career opportunities, including:
- **AI Engineer**: Develop and deploy AI models.
- **Data Scientist**: Analyze data and build predictive models.

- **Machine Learning Engineer**: Focus on designing and optimizing ML algorithms.
- **Research Scientist**: Work on cutting-edge AI research.
- **AI Consultant**: Help businesses implement AI solutions.

With the right skills and experience, you can find opportunities in almost every industry.

Getting started with AI may seem challenging, but with the right resources, practice, and mindset, anyone can learn and excel in this exciting field. Start with the basics, work on projects, and stay curious. Remember, AI is not just about technology—it's about solving problems and creating value. So, take the first step today and unlock the endless possibilities of AI!

14. How ChatGPT Understands Text, Images, and Audio

ChatGPT is more than just a text-based AI—it can generate images, analyze pictures, and even understand audio inputs. But how does it achieve this? The answer lies in the integration of multiple AI models, each specialized for different tasks. In this blog, we'll break down how ChatGPT leverages different AI technologies to create a seamless multimodal experience.

1. Text Understanding and Generation: Powered by GPT-4

At its core, ChatGPT is powered by **GPT-4.** This large language model (LLM) enables ChatGPT to understand and generate human-like text responses.

How GPT-4 Works:

- **Pre-trained on a massive dataset**: GPT-4 has been trained on a vast corpus of text from books, articles, and websites, allowing it to generate coherent and contextually relevant responses.
- **Uses transformers and deep learning**: It processes text using an architecture called a Transformer, which helps in understanding the relationships between words and sentences.
- **Context awareness**: Unlike earlier AI models, GPT-4 maintains context over longer conversations, allowing for more natural interactions.

Applications:

- Answering questions
- Writing and summarizing text
- Generating code
- Assisting in creative writing

---

2. Image Generation: Powered by DALL·E

ChatGPT can generate images based on text descriptions using **DALL·E 3**, a state-of-the-art AI model for image synthesis.

How DALL·E Works:

- **Text-to-Image Model**: It takes a text prompt and converts it into a visual representation.
- **Neural Network Training**: DALL·E is trained on millions of images and their corresponding descriptions, allowing it to create highly detailed and realistic visuals.
- **Inpainting Capabilities**: DALL·E can modify parts of an image while keeping the rest unchanged, useful for refining or editing existing images.

Applications:

- Generating unique artwork
- Designing product mockups
- Creating illustrations for blogs and presentations

3. Audio Understanding: Powered by Whisper

ChatGPT can process and understand speech thanks to **Whisper**, an advanced **Automatic Speech Recognition (ASR)** model developed by OpenAI.

How Whisper Works:

- **Deep learning-based transcription**: Whisper is trained on a vast dataset of spoken language and transcribes speech into text with high accuracy.
- **Multilingual support**: It can recognize and translate multiple languages.
- **Handles background noise**: Unlike traditional ASR systems, Whisper is robust against noisy environments.

Applications:

- Transcribing audio to text
- Converting voice messages into readable content
- Assisting in language translation

4. Image Analysis: GPT-4's Vision Capabilities

ChatGPT isn't just about generating images—it can also **analyze images** and extract meaningful information from them. This is made possible by the **vision capabilities** embedded in GPT-4.

How GPT-4's Vision Model Works:

- **Processes image data**: GPT-4 can interpret visual elements like objects, text, and patterns.
- **Reads text within images**: It can recognize and extract text from screenshots, scanned documents, and handwritten notes.
- **Understands complex visual data**: It can analyze charts, diagrams, and even code snippets within images.

Applications:

- Extracting text from scanned documents
- Identifying objects in images
- Interpreting complex visual data

---

5. How Everything Works Together

ChatGPT acts as a **hub** that connects all these specialized AI models:

- **Text Processing → GPT-4**
- **Image Generation → DALL·E**
- **Audio Processing → Whisper**
- **Image Analysis → GPT-4 Vision**

Whenever you provide an input, ChatGPT determines which model (or combination of models) to use to generate the most relevant response. This seamless integration allows ChatGPT to handle diverse types of input beyond just text.

---

6. Real-World Use Cases of ChatGPT

Beyond understanding and generating content, ChatGPT is widely used in various industries. Here are some of its top applications:

1. Personal Productivity

- Writing Assistance → Drafting emails, reports, essays, and blog posts.
- Summarization → Summarizing articles, books, or meeting notes.
- Brainstorming Ideas → Generating creative ideas for content, projects, or solutions.
- Time Management → Creating schedules, reminders, and to-do lists.

---

2. Business & Professional Use

- Customer Support → AI chatbots for answering FAQs and assisting customers.
- Market Research → Gathering insights, analyzing trends, and summarizing reports.
- Sales & Marketing → Writing ad copy, social media posts, and email campaigns.

- HR & Recruitment → Writing job descriptions and conducting AI-powered screening.

---

3. Education & Learning

- Tutoring → Explaining complex topics in simple terms.
- Language Learning → Practicing conversations and translating text.
- Code Assistance → Debugging, explaining, and generating code snippets.
- Exam Preparation → Providing quizzes and summarizing study materials.

---

4. Content Creation

- Scriptwriting → Generating scripts for videos, podcasts, or plays.
- Storytelling → Writing short stories, poems, or fiction.
- Video Descriptions → Generating YouTube descriptions and captions.
- SEO Optimization → Suggesting keywords and improving blog readability.

---

5. AI & Tech Development

- Coding Help → Generating and explaining code in Python, Java, and more.
- Debugging → Identifying errors and suggesting fixes.
- API Integration → Helping developers use OpenAI's API.
- Database Queries → Writing SQL queries for data retrieval.

---

6. Healthcare & Wellness

- Symptom Checker → Providing general health advice (not a replacement for doctors).
- Mental Health Support → Offering mindfulness exercises and stress management tips.
- Fitness & Diet Planning → Suggesting meal plans and workout routines.
- Medical Research Summaries → Simplifying medical literature for general readers.

---

7. Finance & Investment

- Budgeting Advice → Helping users plan expenses and savings.
- Investment Insights → Summarizing stock market trends (non-financial advice).
- Loan & Credit Information → Explaining loan types, interest rates, and terms.
- Tax Guidance → Providing general tax information and strategies.

---

8. Entertainment & Fun

- Trivia & Quizzes → Creating fun and educational quizzes.
- Game Development → Helping in designing text-based games.
- Jokes & Riddles → Generating jokes, puns, and brain teasers.
- Music Recommendations → Suggesting songs, playlists, and artists.

---

9. Legal & Compliance

- Legal Document Drafting → Writing contracts and agreements (not a substitute for a lawyer).
- Policy & Compliance → Explaining GDPR, data privacy, and cybersecurity policies.
- Intellectual Property Advice → Providing general knowledge on copyrights and trademarks.

---

10. Science & Research

- Explaining Scientific Concepts → Breaking down physics, chemistry, and biology topics.
- Data Analysis → Providing insights from datasets (with user-provided data).
- Research Paper Summarization → Condensing complex research into simple explanations.
- Climate Change Insights → Discussing sustainability and environmental solutions.

ChatGPT is not just a text-based chatbot—it is a **multimodal AI system** that integrates several powerful AI models to understand and generate text, images, and audio. By combining **GPT-4, DALL·E, Whisper, and Vision AI**, it offers a more interactive and versatile experience for users.

As AI continues to evolve, we can expect even more advanced multimodal capabilities, making AI assistants smarter and more intuitive than ever before.

ChatGPT's Memory Feature

ChatGPT's memory feature is revolutionizing the way we interact with AI-powered assistants. By enabling the model to remember information across interactions, it creates a more personalized and context-aware experience. In this chapter, we'll dive deeper into how ChatGPT's memory works, its benefits, how to manage it, and what the future holds for this groundbreaking feature.

What is ChatGPT's Memory Feature?

Traditionally, ChatGPT operated as a stateless AI, meaning it didn't retain any memory of past conversations. Each interaction started with a blank slate, requiring users to reintroduce context or preferences every time. While this approach ensured privacy and simplicity, it often led to repetitive and less efficient conversations.

With the introduction of the memory feature, ChatGPT can now retain information across sessions. This means it can remember details about you, your preferences, and past conversations, creating a more seamless and personalized experience.

How Does ChatGPT's Memory Work?

The memory feature is designed to enhance user experience by making interactions more intuitive and context-aware. Here's how it works in practice:

- **Remembering User Preferences**
  ChatGPT can store details like your name, preferred communication style, or topics of interest. For example, if you mention you're a fan of science fiction, ChatGPT might recommend books or movies in that genre during future interactions.
- **Retaining Past Conversations**
  If you frequently discuss specific subjects—like coding, travel, or fitness—ChatGPT can build on previous discussions. This eliminates the need to re-explain your goals or preferences, saving time and effort.
- **Adapting Responses Over Time**
  The AI refines its responses based on what it learns about you. For instance, if you prefer concise answers, ChatGPT will adapt its tone and length accordingly.
- **Customizing Suggestions**
  Memory enables ChatGPT to offer tailored recommendations. Whether it's suggesting productivity tools, workout routines, or coding resources, the AI can provide more relevant advice based on your history.

Benefits of ChatGPT's Memory Feature

The memory feature offers several advantages that enhance the overall user experience:

- **Enhanced Personalization:** Users no longer need to reintroduce themselves or repeat context. ChatGPT can recall your preferences, making interactions feel more natural and tailored.
- **Improved Efficiency:** By retaining context, ChatGPT reduces redundancy in conversations. This is particularly useful for professionals who rely on the AI for tasks like coding, research, or content creation.
- **Context-Aware Interactions:** ChatGPT can build on past discussions, making responses more coherent and relevant. For example, if you're working on a project, the AI can reference earlier conversations to provide consistent support.
- **Adaptive Learning:** Over time, ChatGPT refines its understanding of your preferences, leading to more accurate and engaging interactions.

Managing ChatGPT's Memory

OpenAI has prioritized user control and transparency with the memory feature. Here's how you can manage it:

- **View What ChatGPT Remembers:** You can check the details ChatGPT has stored about you, ensuring transparency and giving you peace of mind.
- **Turn Memory On or Off:** If you prefer stateless interactions, you can disable the memory feature entirely. This is ideal for users who prioritize privacy or want a fresh start with each session.
- **Delete Specific Entries:** You can remove specific memories if they're no longer relevant or if you want to correct outdated information.
- **Clear All Memory:** A full reset option allows you to erase all stored data, giving you complete control over your interactions.

Privacy and Security Considerations

OpenAI has implemented robust safeguards to ensure the memory feature operates responsibly. Here's how they protect your data:

- **User Notifications**: You'll be notified when ChatGPT updates its memory, keeping you informed about what's being stored.
- **Data Management**: All stored data can be accessed and managed through your settings, giving you full control.
- **Privacy Policies**: OpenAI adheres to strict privacy guidelines to ensure your information is secure and used responsibly.

Future of ChatGPT's Memory

The memory feature is still evolving, and we can expect even more exciting developments in the future. Potential improvements include:

- **Better Context Retention**: The AI could remember longer and more complex conversations, making it even more useful for professional and personal use.
- **Nuanced Understanding**: ChatGPT might develop a deeper understanding of user preferences, enabling more sophisticated personalization.
- **Enhanced Customization**: Future updates could allow users to fine-tune how much and what kind of information ChatGPT remembers.

ChatGPT's memory feature is a significant leap forward in AI-powered assistants. By enabling the model to remember information across interactions, it creates a more personalized, efficient, and context-aware experience. With full user control and transparency, the feature offers flexibility and peace of mind. Whether you prefer a fresh start every session or a chatbot that remembers your preferences, ChatGPT's memory puts the power in your hands.

As AI continues to evolve, features like memory will play a crucial role in making technology more intuitive and human-like. The future of AI-driven assistants is bright, and ChatGPT is leading the way.

15. AI Learning Resources

This guide compiles a comprehensive list of AI resources, spanning machine learning (ML) algorithms, transformer architectures, model fine-tuning, and AI development tools.

If you are reading this from paper book, scan the below QR code to get clickable links.

1. Mastering ML Association Algorithms

AI applications often require discovering patterns in data. Here are some fundamental ML association algorithms:

- **FP-Growth** - Efficiently finds frequent patterns using a tree structure: <u>Learn More</u>
- **Apriori** - Iteratively identifies frequent itemsets, though slower than FP-Growth: <u>Learn More</u>
- **Eclat** - Uses a vertical data format for efficient frequent pattern mining: <u>Learn More</u>

---

2. Understanding AI Model Architectures

General AI Concepts:

- **Gen AI on Edge** - Running AI models on devices instead of the cloud: <u>Explore</u>
- **BERT** - An encoder-only model for text classification: <u>Read the Paper</u>
- **Emergent Tasks** - Discovering unexpected abilities in large models: <u>Explained Here</u>
- **Encoding Models** - Understanding text representations: <u>Learn More</u>
- **Sentence Transformers** - Converting text into vector representations: <u>Explore</u>

3. Essential Activation Functions in Neural Networks

Activation functions are key in neural networks, defining how signals pass through layers.

- **Linear** - Simple but rarely used: Test It
- **ReLU** - Efficient, though neurons can "die": Try It
- **Leaky ReLU** - Fixes dead ReLU issues: Read More
- **ELU** - Avoids dying gradients: Learn More
- **Swish** - A smooth alternative to ReLU: Explore
- **Softmax** - Converts outputs into probabilities for classification: Understand It

4. AI Model Fine-Tuning Techniques

Fine-tuning pre-trained models is crucial for domain-specific AI applications.

- **Supervised Fine-Tuning** - Training on labeled datasets: Learn More
- **Parameter-Efficient Fine-Tuning (PEFT)** - Optimizing specific model parameters: Check This
- **Instruction Tuning** - Enhancing model adaptability: Overview
- **Pruning** - Reducing model size while maintaining accuracy: Read More

5. AI Development Tools & Workbenches

Experimentation and model development require powerful tools. Here are some popular ones:

- **Google Colab** - Free cloud-based Python notebooks with GPU support: Explore
- **AWS SageMaker** - Scalable ML model deployment: Learn More
- **Hugging Face Pipelines** - Easy model deployment: Try It
- **LangChain** - A framework for developing AI applications: Start Here

6. AI Model Serving & Deployment

Deploying AI models efficiently ensures real-time inference and scalability.

- **Kserve** - Kubernetes-based model serving: <u>Check It Out</u>
- **Ray Serve** - Scalable ML model inference: <u>Learn More</u>
- **NVIDIA TensorRT LLM** - Optimized serving for NVIDIA GPUs: <u>Read More</u>
- **vLLM** - High-speed large language model serving: <u>Explore</u>

---

7. AI Coding Assistants

Accelerate your AI development with AI-powered code assistants.

- **GitHub Copilot** - AI pair programmer: <u>Try It</u>
- **Amazon Q** - AWS AI-powered coding assistant: <u>Learn More</u>
- **Codeium** - Free AI-powered code completion: <u>Check It Out</u>
- **Cursor** - AI-powered code editor: <u>Explore</u>

---

8. AI App Prototyping & Sandboxing

Rapidly prototype AI applications with these tools.

- **Gradio** - Easy UI creation for ML models: <u>Start Here</u>
- **Streamlit** - Python-based data app framework: <u>Explore</u>
- **FastHTML** - Quick HTML prototyping for AI applications: <u>Try It</u>
- **Sandboxing** - Securely isolate AI models: <u>Read More</u>

16. Hugging Face: Revolutionizing Natural Language Processing and AI Development

In the rapidly evolving world of Artificial Intelligence, one name stands out as a game-changer – **Hugging Face**. If you're into Natural Language Processing (NLP) or just curious about how cutting-edge language models like GPT and BERT work, then Hugging Face is a platform you need to know about. But what exactly is Hugging Face, and why is it creating such a buzz in the AI community?

Let's dive deep into the world of Hugging Face, exploring its history, key features, popular models, and how it's empowering developers and researchers worldwide.

1. What is Hugging Face?

Hugging Face started as a chatbot company in 2016 but quickly pivoted to become the leading platform for **Natural Language Processing (NLP)**. It's now known for its open-source **Transformers library**, which has become the go-to resource for building state-of-the-art NLP applications.

Hugging Face provides a vast ecosystem, including:

- **Transformers Library:** A collection of pre-trained models for NLP tasks like text classification, translation, summarization, and more.
- **Datasets Library:** An easy-to-use hub for accessing and sharing datasets.
- **Model Hub:** A community-driven repository with thousands of pre-trained models.
- **Inference API and Spaces:** Tools for deploying models and creating interactive demos.

Whether you're a researcher, data scientist, or developer, Hugging Face makes it easier than ever to **build, train, and deploy NLP models**.

---

2. Key Features and Components
A. Transformers Library

The **Transformers library** is the heart of Hugging Face's ecosystem. It supports popular architectures like:

- **BERT (Bidirectional Encoder Representations from Transformers)** – For text classification and question answering.
- **GPT (Generative Pre-trained Transformer)** – For text generation and conversational AI.
- **T5 (Text-To-Text Transfer Transformer)** – For versatile text-to-text tasks like summarization and translation.
- **RoBERTa, DistilBERT, Electra, and more** – Optimized models for faster inference and better performance.

With just a few lines of code, you can **load pre-trained models** or **fine-tune them on custom datasets**. Here's how easy it is to get started:

```
from transformers import pipeline

# Load a sentiment analysis pipeline
classifier = pipeline('sentiment-analysis')
```

```
# Analyze sentiment of a sentence
result = classifier("I love using Hugging Face!")
print(result)
```

This simplicity and flexibility are what make Hugging Face a favorite among AI enthusiasts and professionals alike.

B. Model Hub

The **Model Hub** is a community-driven repository with over **100,000 pre-trained models** contributed by researchers, companies, and developers worldwide. You can:

- **Explore models** for various tasks, including text classification, question answering, summarization, translation, and image classification.
- **Upload your own models** to share with the community.
- **Directly integrate models** into your projects using the Transformers library.

This open and collaborative ecosystem accelerates research and application development, enabling users to **build on top of state-of-the-art models** without reinventing the wheel.

C. Datasets Library

The **Datasets Library** offers a wide range of datasets for NLP tasks, including:

- Text classification (e.g., IMDb, AG News)
- Question answering (e.g., SQuAD, TriviaQA)
- Machine translation (e.g., WMT datasets)
- Summarization (e.g., CNN/Daily Mail)

With seamless integration, you can **load datasets directly into your machine learning pipelines** using this simple code:

```
from datasets import load_dataset

# Load the IMDb dataset for text classification
dataset = load_dataset("imdb")
print(dataset)
```

This streamlined approach to data handling makes it easier for researchers and developers to **experiment with new ideas and iterate faster**.

D. Inference API and Spaces

- **Inference API:** A cloud-based service that allows you to deploy models as APIs without worrying about infrastructure.
- **Spaces:** An interactive platform for creating and sharing ML demos using Gradio or Streamlit.

This makes Hugging Face a complete end-to-end solution, from model development to deployment and demonstration.

---

3. Popular Use Cases

Hugging Face is being used across industries for a wide range of applications, including:

1. **Text Classification:** Sentiment analysis, spam detection, and topic categorization.
2. **Conversational AI:** Building intelligent chatbots and virtual assistants.
3. **Question Answering:** Creating knowledge retrieval systems for customer support and educational platforms.
4. **Text Summarization and Translation:** Efficient content generation for news, marketing, and global communication.
5. **Research and Academia:** Rapid prototyping and experimentation with state-of-the-art NLP models.

With its **intuitive interface and extensive documentation**, Hugging Face is perfect for both beginners and advanced users.

---

4. Why Choose Hugging Face?

- **Open Source and Community Driven:** Contributed by researchers and developers worldwide, fostering innovation and collaboration.
- **State-of-the-Art Models:** Access to cutting-edge NLP models with continuous updates and improvements.
- **Ease of Use:** Intuitive APIs and extensive documentation make it beginner-friendly.
- **End-to-End Ecosystem:** From datasets and model development to deployment and demo creation.
- **Scalable and Production-Ready:** Seamless integration with cloud platforms like AWS, GCP, and Azure.

Whether you're a data scientist looking to build custom NLP solutions or a developer wanting to integrate AI into your application, Hugging Face **empowers you to achieve more with less effort**.

---

5. Getting Started with Hugging Face

Ready to explore Hugging Face? Here's how to get started:

1. **Visit the Website:** Hugging Face to explore the Model Hub and Datasets.
2. **Install the Transformers Library:**
   pip install transformers
3. **Join the Community:** Connect with AI enthusiasts and experts on the Hugging Face Forum and Discord.
4. **Follow Tutorials:** Check out the Hugging Face Course to learn how to use the platform effectively.

---

6. Conclusion: The Future of NLP with Hugging Face

Hugging Face has revolutionized the way we build and deploy NLP applications. By democratizing access to state-of-the-art models and fostering a collaborative community, it's paving the way for the **next generation of AI solutions**.

Whether you're an NLP researcher, AI enthusiast, or developer, Hugging Face empowers you to **innovate faster, build smarter, and reach new heights in AI development**.

So, what are you waiting for? **Dive into the world of Hugging Face today and start building the AI solutions of tomorrow!**

17. LangChain: Revolutionizing LLM-Powered Applications

In the world of AI and Natural Language Processing (NLP), the rise of large language models (LLMs) like GPT-4, PaLM, and Claude has been groundbreaking. These models exhibit remarkable capabilities in generating human-like text, answering questions, translating languages, and much more. But leveraging them efficiently for real-world applications involves several challenges, including memory management, contextual awareness, and integration with external data sources.

Enter **LangChain**, an innovative framework designed to bridge these gaps and empower developers to build powerful LLM-driven applications with enhanced capabilities. In this blog post, we will explore what LangChain is, its key features, and how it is revolutionizing the landscape of LLM-powered solutions.

What is LangChain?

LangChain is an open-source framework built to facilitate the development of complex applications powered by large language models. It goes beyond merely generating text by enabling:

- **Long-term Memory:** Maintaining conversational context across interactions.
- **External Data Integration:** Connecting LLMs with APIs, databases, and other data sources.
- **Advanced Prompt Engineering:** Modular and reusable prompts for consistent performance.
- **Tool Utilization:** Integrating external tools like calculators, search engines, and more.

With LangChain, developers can build chatbots, personal assistants, search engines, and a variety of other LLM-powered applications that require dynamic, context-aware interactions.

Why Use LangChain?

1. **Stateful Conversations:** Unlike traditional LLMs that are stateless, LangChain enables long-term memory, making it ideal for building conversational AI applications with context retention.
2. **Seamless Integration:** Easily integrate with external data sources such as APIs, vector stores, and databases, ensuring that the model has access to up-to-date information.
3. **Modular Design:** LangChain is built with modularity in mind, allowing developers to mix and match components to build customized workflows.
4. **Prompt Management:** Advanced prompt templates and chains for consistent and optimized model performance.
5. **Tool Utilization:** Equips LLMs with external tools for enhanced functionalities like calculations, real-time information retrieval, and more.

Core Components of LangChain

LangChain's architecture is built around six core components:

1. LLMs

LLMs are the core engines behind LangChain. It supports various models, including OpenAI's GPT-4, Anthropic's Claude, Google's PaLM, and local models like Llama 2.

Example: Initializing OpenAI's GPT-4 model:

```
from langchain.llms import OpenAI
llm = OpenAI(model_name="gpt-4", temperature=0.7)
response = llm("What are the latest trends in AI?")
print(response)
```

Note: As langchain is frequently changing its libraries and rearranging its packages, you may need to make changes in the sample codes to make it work.

---

2. Prompts

Prompts are the instructions given to the LLMs. LangChain offers **PromptTemplates** that allow you to create modular and reusable prompts.

Example: Creating a prompt template:

```python
from langchain.prompts import PromptTemplate

template = PromptTemplate(
    input_variables=["product"],
    template="Write a catchy advertisement for {product}."
)

prompt = template.format(product="smartwatch")
print(prompt)
```

Output:

"Write a catchy advertisement for smartwatch."

This modular approach ensures consistency and efficiency when working with complex prompt structures.

---

3. Chains

Chains allow you to link multiple components together. This is useful when you need to perform sequential tasks, such as question-answering followed by a summary.

Example: Creating a simple LLM chain:

```python
from langchain.chains import LLMChain

llm_chain = LLMChain(llm=llm, prompt=template)
output = llm_chain.run(product="smartwatch")
print(output)
```

---

4. Memory

One of LangChain's standout features is its memory capability, which allows LLMs to maintain context across interactions. This is essential for building conversational agents.

Example: Adding conversational memory:

```
from langchain.chains import ConversationChain
from langchain.memory import ConversationBufferMemory

memory = ConversationBufferMemory()
conversation = ConversationChain(llm=llm, memory=memory)

conversation.predict(input="Hello!")
conversation.predict(input="What's the weather today?")
```

The model retains context, allowing for more natural and coherent conversations.

---

5. Indexes

Indexes allow LLMs to retrieve relevant information from large datasets or documents. LangChain integrates seamlessly with vector stores like Pinecone, Chroma, and FAISS for efficient document retrieval.

Example: Setting up a vector store index:

```
from langchain.vectorstores import Chroma
from langchain.embeddings import OpenAIEmbeddings

embeddings = OpenAIEmbeddings()
vector_store = Chroma(persist_directory="data/indexes",
embedding_function=embeddings)
```

This enables the model to fetch contextually relevant documents, enhancing accuracy in information retrieval tasks.

---

6. Agents and Tools

Agents enable LLMs to interact with external tools like search engines, calculators, APIs, and more. This significantly expands their functional scope.

Example: Using an agent with a search tool:

```
from langchain.agents import initialize_agent, Tool
from langchain.tools import SerpAPIWrapper

search = SerpAPIWrapper()
tools = [Tool(name="search", func=search.run, description="Search the
web")]
```

```
agent = initialize_agent(tools, llm,
agent_type="zero-shot-react-description", verbose=True)
response = agent("Who won the FIFA World Cup in 2022?")
print(response)
```

Here, the agent utilizes the SerpAPI tool to retrieve real-time information, making the model more dynamic and useful in real-world scenarios.

Real-World Applications of LangChain

LangChain's versatile components enable the development of various applications, including:

- **Intelligent Chatbots:** Stateful and context-aware virtual assistants.
- **Customer Support Automation:** Personalized and dynamic support systems.
- **Document Search Engines:** Contextual search over vast document repositories.
- **Content Generation:** Advanced content generation workflows with prompt engineering.
- **Recommendation Systems:** Personalized recommendations using memory and indexing.

Why Choose LangChain Over Traditional Approaches?

Traditional LLM implementations are typically stateless and limited in terms of external data integration. LangChain addresses these limitations by:

- Enabling contextual conversations with long-term memory.
- Allowing dynamic data fetching through integrated tools and APIs.
- Facilitating complex workflows using Chains.
- Offering advanced prompt management for consistent performance.

These features make LangChain a superior choice for building robust, real-world applications powered by large language models.

Conclusion: The Future of LLM-Powered Applications

LangChain is revolutionizing the way developers build and deploy LLM-powered applications. Its modular and flexible architecture empowers developers to create dynamic, context-aware solutions with minimal effort. Whether you're building a conversational agent, a custom search engine, or an intelligent content generator, LangChain provides all the building blocks needed to bring your vision to life.

Get Started Today!

To start building with LangChain, check out the Official Documentation and explore its capabilities. As LLMs continue to evolve, LangChain stands at the forefront of enabling innovative and intelligent applications.

18. Understanding Input Window Limitation in Large Language Models (LLMs)

Large Language Models (LLMs) like GPT-4 and Claude are transforming natural language processing, enabling sophisticated text generation and complex conversations. However, one fundamental constraint that influences their functionality and performance is the **input window limitation**. In this chapter, we'll explore what this limitation is, how it works, its impact on performance, and strategies to optimize LLM usage effectively.

What is the Input Window in LLMs?

The input window, also known as the context window, is the maximum amount of text (measured in tokens) that an LLM can process in a single interaction. Tokens can be as short as one character or as long as one word, depending on the language and complexity. For instance, the word "hello" is one token, while a complex sentence can be several tokens.

This limitation defines how much context the model can retain at once. If the input or conversation exceeds this window, older tokens are truncated or "forgotten," affecting the model's continuity and coherence.

Why Does Input Window Limitation Matter?

The input window limitation impacts several key aspects of LLM functionality:

1. **Context Retention:** LLMs can only "remember" the text within the current window. If the conversation or text exceeds this limit, earlier parts are lost, leading to context discontinuity.
2. **Long-Form Content Generation:** Generating lengthy articles, stories, or detailed technical explanations becomes challenging because the model can't maintain full context throughout the output.

3. **Complex Conversations:** In detailed discussions, maintaining coherence is difficult if the input window is exceeded, leading to incomplete or repetitive answers.

How Does the Input Window Affect Performance?

Input window limitations are closely tied to the performance and efficiency of LLMs in the following ways:

1. Memory and Contextual Understanding:
   - LLMs can only consider the information within their input window. This affects context retention, making it challenging to maintain continuity in long conversations or documents.
   - Truncated context can lead to inconsistent or repetitive outputs, affecting user experience and the perceived intelligence of the model.
2. Inference Speed and Computational Efficiency:
   - Larger input windows require more computational resources and memory. The model's inference speed decreases as the number of tokens increases.
   - This is because transformers (the architecture behind most LLMs) process input tokens in parallel, leading to quadratic time complexity concerning the sequence length.
3. Accuracy and Coherence of Output:
   - If context is lost due to input window constraints, the model's responses can become less accurate or relevant.
   - In narrative tasks, this can result in plot inconsistencies or abrupt style changes. In technical writing, it may lead to fragmented or disjointed explanations.
4. Resource Utilization and Cost:
   - Processing longer inputs requires more GPU/TPU resources, increasing operational costs. This is particularly relevant for enterprises deploying LLMs at scale.
   - Memory usage scales with input size, impacting hardware requirements and infrastructure scalability.

Input Window Sizes in Popular LLMs

Different LLMs come with varying input window sizes:

- **GPT-3:** ~4,096 tokens (~3,000 words) – Suitable for short to medium-length tasks but struggles with long-form content.
- **GPT-4:** Available in 8k and 32k token versions (~6,000 and ~24,000 words, respectively). The 32k version provides enhanced context retention but is slower and more resource-intensive.
- **Claude (Anthropic's LLM):** Offers up to 100k tokens, ideal for maintaining extensive context but comes with higher latency and cost.

Trade-offs and Challenges

Increasing the input window size can improve context retention and output coherence but introduces certain trade-offs:

- **Higher Computational Load:** More tokens require more processing power and memory.
- **Diminishing Returns:** Beyond a certain point, increasing the window size yields minimal performance gains, as not all tokens contribute equally to context.
- **Cost Implications:** Larger models with bigger input windows are costlier to deploy and maintain.

Strategies to Manage Input Window Limitations

To effectively work within input window constraints while optimizing performance, consider the following strategies:

1. Context Pruning and Summarization:
    - Remove less relevant parts of the conversation while preserving essential context.
    - Summarize earlier parts to retain continuity without exceeding the input window.
2. Chunking Strategy:
    - Break down long inputs into smaller, manageable chunks and process them sequentially.

- Maintain context by summarizing or selectively carrying over relevant information between chunks.

3. Retrieval-Augmented Generation (RAG):
   - Combine LLMs with external knowledge bases, reducing the dependency on large input windows by fetching relevant information on demand.
   - This approach enhances accuracy and contextual relevance without overwhelming the input window.

4. Hierarchical Memory:
   - Implement hierarchical architectures where only summary-level information is retained in the input window.
   - This approach balances context retention with computational efficiency.

The Future of Input Window Limitations

Researchers are actively exploring ways to expand input window sizes and optimize performance. Some key advancements include:

- **Efficient Transformers:** New architectures designed to reduce computational complexity and memory usage.
- **Memory-Augmented Networks:** Models that retain context across interactions without relying solely on the input window.
- **Hierarchical Transformers:** Techniques that manage context at different granularities, improving long-term coherence.

As technology evolves, we can expect larger input windows and more efficient architectures, paving the way for more coherent and contextually aware AI models.

The input window limitation is a critical factor influencing the performance of LLMs, impacting context retention, accuracy, inference speed, and computational cost. By understanding and strategically managing this limitation, users can maximize the effectiveness of LLMs in real-world applications.

Whether you are developing a conversational AI system, generating long-form content, or building complex decision-making models, managing input window constraints is essential for optimal performance. As LLM architectures continue to evolve, innovative solutions are expected to redefine the boundaries of what's possible, making LLMs more powerful and contextually intelligent than ever before.

19. Understanding Computer Vision

Computer Vision is a field of artificial intelligence that enables machines to interpret and understand the visual world. By analyzing images, videos, and other visual inputs, computer vision systems can perform tasks like image recognition, object detection, facial recognition, and even autonomous navigation. From self-driving cars to medical imaging and augmented reality, computer vision is revolutionizing how machines perceive and interact with the world around us.

In this blog post, we will explore the fundamental concepts of computer vision, its techniques, applications, challenges, and the latest trends shaping the future of this fascinating technology.

What is Computer Vision?

Computer Vision is the science and technology of enabling machines to understand and interpret visual data. It involves teaching computers to recognize patterns, detect objects, and make decisions based on images and videos. By mimicking the human visual system, computer vision systems aim to achieve human-like perception, enabling machines to see, understand, and interact with their environment.

The ultimate goal of computer vision is to create systems that can perform visual tasks autonomously, ranging from basic image classification to complex scene understanding and real-time action recognition.

How Does Computer Vision Work?

At its core, computer vision relies on a combination of image processing, machine learning, and deep learning algorithms. Here's a simplified overview of the process:

1. **Image Acquisition:** Capturing images or videos using cameras, sensors, or other imaging devices.

2. **Pre-processing:** Enhancing image quality by removing noise, adjusting brightness, or resizing.

3. **Feature Extraction:** Identifying important features such as edges, corners, textures, and colors.

4. **Object Detection and Recognition:** Locating objects within the image and classifying them into predefined categories.

5. **Post-processing and Decision Making:** Interpreting the results and taking necessary actions based on the analysis.

Modern computer vision systems heavily rely on **deep learning** techniques, especially **Convolutional Neural Networks (CNNs)**, which are highly effective in learning hierarchical patterns from visual data.

Key Techniques in Computer Vision

1. Image Classification
   - Identifying the primary category or class of an image (e.g., cat, dog, car).
   - Popular models: **ResNet**, **VGGNet**, and **EfficientNet**.

2. Object Detection
   - Locating and identifying multiple objects within an image along with their bounding boxes.
   - Popular models: **YOLO (You Only Look Once)**, **Faster R-CNN**, and **SSD (Single Shot MultiBox Detector)**.

3. Image Segmentation
   - Dividing an image into meaningful regions or segments for detailed analysis.
   - Types: **Semantic Segmentation** (classifying each pixel) and **Instance Segmentation** (differentiating individual instances).
   - Popular models: **Mask R-CNN**, **U-Net**, and **DeepLab**.

4. Facial Recognition and Analysis
   - Identifying and verifying human faces for authentication or surveillance.

- Used in security systems, social media tagging, and emotion detection.

5. Optical Character Recognition (OCR)

   - Converting text in images or scanned documents into machine-readable text.

   - Applications include document digitization and license plate recognition.

6. Pose Estimation and Action Recognition

   - Estimating human body poses and recognizing actions in videos.

   - Used in sports analytics, gaming, and human-computer interaction.

Applications of Computer Vision

1. Autonomous Vehicles

   - Computer vision enables self-driving cars to perceive their surroundings, detect obstacles, read traffic signs, and navigate safely.

   - Key technologies: **LIDAR**, **Radar**, and **Camera-based Object Detection**.

2. Healthcare and Medical Imaging

   - Assisting radiologists in diagnosing diseases from medical images (e.g., X-rays, MRIs, and CT scans).

   - Applications include cancer detection, retinal disease screening, and surgical assistance.

3. Retail and E-commerce

   - Visual search, virtual try-on, and personalized product recommendations using image recognition.

   - In-store analytics for inventory management and customer behavior tracking.

4. Security and Surveillance

   - Facial recognition systems for authentication and public safety.

   - Anomaly detection for identifying suspicious activities in real-time.

5. Augmented Reality (AR) and Virtual Reality (VR)

   - Computer vision powers immersive experiences by accurately tracking user movements.

   - Applications include AR filters, virtual shopping, and gaming.

6. Agriculture and Environmental Monitoring

- ○ Crop health monitoring using drone-based imagery analysis.
- ○ Environmental monitoring for wildlife conservation and climate change analysis.

Challenges in Computer Vision

1. Data Privacy and Security
   - ○ Facial recognition systems raise concerns about privacy and surveillance.
   - ○ Ensuring data security and ethical usage is crucial for responsible deployment.
2. Data Quality and Bias
   - ○ Performance heavily depends on the quality and diversity of training data.
   - ○ Bias in datasets can lead to inaccurate or unfair outcomes.
3. Real-Time Processing
   - ○ High computational power is required for real-time video analysis and inference.
   - ○ Efficient edge computing solutions are needed for deployment on mobile devices.
4. Generalization and Robustness
   - ○ Models must generalize well to new environments, lighting conditions, and perspectives.
   - ○ Adversarial attacks can fool models into making incorrect predictions.

Latest Trends and Future Directions

1. Self-Supervised Learning
   - ○ Learning meaningful visual representations without extensive labeled datasets.
   - ○ Models like **SimCLR** and **MAE (Masked Autoencoders)** are leading the way.
2. Vision Transformers (ViTs)
   - ○ Transformers, originally designed for NLP, are now being applied to vision tasks.
   - ○ Vision Transformers (e.g., **ViT**, **Swin Transformer**) offer state-of-the-art performance in classification and segmentation.
3. Multi-Modal Learning
   - ○ Combining visual and textual data for more comprehensive understanding.
   - ○ Example: **CLIP (Contrastive Language-Image Pre-training)** by OpenAI.

Rajamanickam.Com

4. Edge AI and Real-Time Inference
   - Deploying computer vision models on edge devices for low-latency applications.
   - Popular frameworks: **TensorFlow Lite**, **ONNX Runtime**, and **NVIDIA TensorRT**.
5. Ethical AI and Fairness
   - Addressing ethical concerns and biases in facial recognition and surveillance systems.
   - Ensuring transparency, fairness, and accountability in AI systems.

Popular Tools and Frameworks

- **OpenCV** – Open-source computer vision library for image processing and real-time applications.
- **TensorFlow and PyTorch** – Deep learning frameworks widely used for training vision models.
- **Detectron2** – Facebook AI's framework for object detection and segmentation.
- **MMDetection and YOLOv8** – State-of-the-art libraries for object detection.
- **Hugging Face Transformers** – Supporting Vision Transformers and multi-modal models.

Computer vision is transforming industries and enhancing human-machine interactions by enabling machines to see, understand, and respond to visual information. From autonomous vehicles to healthcare diagnostics, augmented reality, and security systems, the possibilities are limitless.

As deep learning architectures evolve and computational power increases, computer vision systems will continue to achieve human-like perception and reasoning. However, addressing challenges like data privacy, bias, and real-time processing is crucial for responsible and ethical deployment.

The future of computer vision is exciting, with advancements in **Vision Transformers**, **Self-Supervised Learning**, and **Multi-Modal Models** paving the way for more intelligent and context-aware systems. Whether you're a beginner or an expert, diving into computer vision offers endless opportunities for innovation and impact.

20. A Beginner's Guide to Training an AI Model

AI and machine learning have become more accessible than ever, thanks to frameworks like TensorFlow. In this guide, we'll walk through the basics of training an AI model using a dataset and explain how to use the trained model.

Getting Started with AI Model Training

If you are new to AI, it is important to start with an overview before diving into complex details. We will use **TensorFlow**, a popular machine-learning framework developed by Google. You can explore TensorFlow resources at tensorflow.org, where many tutorials and pre-built examples are available.

Running AI Code in Google Colab

Google Colab provides a free cloud-based environment for running Python notebooks. You don't need to install anything on your computer, and Google provides the necessary computing resources, including RAM and GPU. To get started:

1. Visit colab.google.com in your web browser.
2. Open a new notebook (.ipynb file).
3. Add code cells to run Python code and text cells for explanations.

A Simple AI Model Using TensorFlow

Let's use TensorFlow and Keras to train a basic AI model. The example provided on TensorFlow's homepage loads a dataset, builds a neural network model, trains it, and evaluates its accuracy.

Step 1: Import Required Libraries

```
import tensorflow as tf
from tensorflow import keras
import matplotlib.pyplot as plt
```

Step 2: Load the Dataset

We will use the **MNIST dataset**, a collection of handwritten digits (0-9). This dataset has 60,000 training images and 10,000 test images.

```
mnist = keras.datasets.mnist
(train_images, train_labels), (test_images, test_labels) =
mnist.load_data()
```

Step 3: Normalize the Data

Neural networks perform better when inputs are scaled between 0 and 1.

```
train_images, test_images = train_images / 255.0, test_images / 255.0
```

Step 4: Build the Model

We define a simple neural network with an input layer, a hidden layer, and an output layer.

```
model = keras.Sequential([
    keras.layers.Flatten(input_shape=(28, 28)),
    keras.layers.Dense(128, activation='relu'),
    keras.layers.Dense(10, activation='softmax')
])
```

Step 5: Compile and Train the Model

We specify the optimizer, loss function, and metrics, then train the model using the dataset.

```
model.compile(optimizer='adam',
              loss='sparse_categorical_crossentropy',
              metrics=['accuracy'])
model.fit(train_images, train_labels, epochs=5)
```

Step 6: Evaluate the Model

Once trained, we can test the model's accuracy using the test dataset.

```
test_loss, test_acc = model.evaluate(test_images, test_labels)
print(f'Test accuracy: {test_acc}')
```

Using the model/Prediction

```
predictions = model.predict(x_test)
predicted_label = np.argmax(predictions[0])
plt.imshow(x_test[0], cmap='gray')
plt.title(f'Predicted: {predicted_label}')
plt.show()
```

Training an AI model is a straightforward process when using TensorFlow and Google Colab. This example provides a basic introduction, but you can explore more advanced techniques as you gain experience. Try modifying the model architecture or experimenting with different datasets to deepen your understanding!

21. Natural Language Processing (NLP)

Natural Language Processing (NLP) is a branch of <u>artificial intelligence</u> that focuses on the interaction between computers and human language. It enables machines to read, understand, and generate human language, bridging the communication gap between humans and computers. From voice assistants to chatbots, NLP is transforming the way we interact with technology.

How Does NLP Work?

NLP combines computational linguistics with machine learning algorithms to process and interpret text and speech. It involves several key steps:

1. **Tokenization:** Breaking down text into smaller units like words or phrases.
2. **Part-of-Speech Tagging:** Identifying the grammatical category of words.
3. **Named Entity Recognition (NER):** Detecting and categorizing entities like names, dates, and locations.
4. **Sentiment Analysis:** Analyzing emotions and opinions expressed in text.
5. **Language Generation:** Producing human-like text or speech output.

Real-World Applications of NLP

1. **Chatbots and Virtual Assistants:** Powering conversational agents like Siri, Alexa, and ChatGPT.
2. **Sentiment Analysis:** Helping businesses understand customer opinions on social media and reviews.
3. **Machine Translation:** Enabling language translation tools like Google Translate.
4. **Text Summarization:** Automatically generating summaries from long articles or reports.
5. **Voice Recognition:** Converting spoken language into text for voice-controlled devices.

NLP Challenges and Limitations

Despite its advancements, NLP faces challenges like:

- **Ambiguity and Context:** Words can have multiple meanings depending on context.
- **Sarcasm and Humor Detection:** Difficulties in interpreting sarcasm, irony, and humor.
- **Bias in Language Models:** Risk of biased outputs due to training data limitations.

The Future of NLP

With rapid advancements in deep learning and transformer architectures (like GPT and BERT), the future of NLP looks promising. We can expect more accurate language models, improved contextual understanding, and seamless human-computer interactions.

22. Mastering Prompt Engineering: The Art and Science of Communicating with AI

In the world of **AI** and natural language processing (NLP), prompt engineering has emerged as a crucial skill for maximizing the potential of large language models (LLMs) like OpenAI's GPT, Google's Gemini, and Anthropic's Claude. As these models become more powerful and versatile, the ability to craft effective prompts can significantly influence the quality, relevance, and accuracy of the generated output.

But what exactly is prompt engineering? Why is it so important? And how can you master the art of writing prompts to get the best out of AI models? In this comprehensive guide, we will explore the fundamentals of prompt engineering, best practices, challenges, and advanced techniques to help you become a pro at communicating with AI.

What is Prompt Engineering?

Prompt engineering is the process of designing and refining input queries (or prompts) to elicit the most accurate, relevant, and useful responses from AI language models. It involves crafting questions, statements, or commands in a way that maximizes the model's performance and minimizes ambiguity or bias.

In essence, prompt engineering is about knowing **what to ask**, **how to ask**, and **how to guide** the model to produce the desired output. It is both an art and a science, requiring creativity, critical thinking, and an understanding of the model's behavior.

Why is Prompt Engineering Important?

1. **Maximizing Model Performance**: The quality of the output is highly dependent on the input. A well-crafted prompt can lead to more accurate, coherent, and contextually relevant responses.
2. **Reducing Bias and Ambiguity**: Clear and precise prompts help minimize biases and ambiguities in the model's output.
3. **Efficiency and Productivity**: Effective prompts reduce the need for multiple iterations, saving time and computational resources.
4. **Customizing Outputs**: By tailoring prompts, users can customize the tone, style, and format of the output to suit specific needs (e.g., formal reports, creative writing, or technical explanations).
5. **Enhancing User Experience**: In applications like chatbots, search engines, and virtual assistants, prompt engineering enhances user interactions and satisfaction.

Core Principles of Prompt Engineering

1. Clarity and Specificity

- Be clear and specific about the information you want. Avoid vague or overly general prompts.
- Example: Instead of asking, "Tell me about space," ask, "Explain the process of star formation in simple terms."

2. Context and Background
   - Provide necessary context to guide the model's understanding of the query.
   - Example: "As a high school science student, explain how photosynthesis works in plants."

3. Task Instruction and Constraints
   - Clearly define the task and any constraints such as word limit, format, or style.
   - Example: "Summarize this article in 100 words using bullet points."

4. Incremental Prompting
   - Break down complex questions into smaller, manageable parts.
   - Example: "First, explain what black holes are. Then, describe how they form."

5. Iteration and Refinement
   - Continuously refine the prompt based on the output received to achieve the desired result.
   - Example: If the output is too detailed, modify the prompt to request a brief summary.

Types of Prompts

1. Zero-Shot Prompts
   - Directly ask the model to perform a task without any examples.
   - Example: "Translate this sentence into French: 'How are you today?'"

2. One-Shot Prompts
   - Provide one example to guide the model's response.
   - Example: "Translate the following sentences into Spanish. Example: 'Hello' -> 'Hola'. Now translate: 'Good morning.'"

3. Few-Shot Prompts
   - Include multiple examples to provide more context and guidance.

- Example: "Translate the following sentences into Japanese. 'Thank you' -> 'Arigatou'. 'Good night' -> 'Oyasuminasai'. Now translate: 'Goodbye.'"

4. Chain-of-Thought Prompts
   - Encourage the model to think through a problem step by step.
   - Example: "Solve this math problem step by step: If $3x + 5 = 20$, what is the value of x?"

5. Instruction-Based Prompts
   - Provide detailed instructions to guide the model's behavior.
   - Example: "Write a formal email to request a meeting with the project manager. Be polite and concise."

Advanced Prompt Engineering Techniques

1. Role Playing and Persona Assignment
   - Assign a role or persona to the model to get context-specific responses.
   - Example: "You are a history professor. Explain the causes of World War II."

2. Contextual Memory and Continuity
   - Maintain context across multiple interactions for coherent conversations.
   - Example: In chatbots, reference earlier parts of the conversation for continuity.

3. Bias Mitigation and Safety
   - Use disclaimers or neutral phrasing to reduce bias and ensure safe outputs.
   - Example: "Provide an unbiased summary of the political debate without personal opinions."

4. Prompt Chaining
   - Use a series of interconnected prompts to achieve complex tasks.
   - Example: First, summarize a long document. Then, extract key insights from the summary.

Challenges in Prompt Engineering

1. Ambiguity and Misinterpretation

- The model may misinterpret vague prompts, leading to irrelevant outputs.

2. Bias and Fairness

- Models can inadvertently reflect biases present in the training data.

3. Creativity vs. Control

- Balancing creative outputs with controlled, accurate information is challenging.

4. Prompt Sensitivity

- Small changes in wording can significantly impact the model's response.

5. Context Limitation

- Current models have context length limitations, affecting continuity in long conversations.

Best Practices for Effective Prompt Engineering

- **Experiment and Iterate**: Continuously experiment with different phrasings and structures.
- **Be Specific and Direct**: Clear instructions lead to more relevant outputs.
- **Use Examples Strategically**: Guide the model with few-shot or one-shot examples.
- **Test for Bias and Safety**: Validate prompts to avoid biased or harmful outputs.
- **Balance Creativity and Accuracy**: Adjust prompts to balance creative freedom and factual accuracy.

Tools and Platforms for Prompt Engineering

1. **OpenAI Playground** – Interactive environment to experiment with GPT models.
2. **Hugging Face Transformers** – Framework for fine-tuning and experimenting with custom prompts.
3. **Prompt Engineering Libraries** – Tools like LangChain for designing and optimizing prompts.
4. **AI21 Studio and Cohere** – Platforms for building NLP applications with custom prompt designs.

With the rapid advancement of LLMs, the field of prompt engineering is evolving. Here are some trends shaping its future:

- **Automated Prompt Generation**: Using AI to optimize and generate prompts dynamically.
- **Multimodal Prompting**: Combining text, images, and audio in a single prompt.
- **Contextual Awareness**: Models becoming more context-aware, requiring less explicit guidance.
- **Ethical Prompt Design**: Developing guidelines for responsible and ethical prompt engineering.

Prompt engineering is a powerful and essential skill for harnessing the full potential of large language models. By mastering the art of crafting effective prompts, you can unlock unparalleled creativity, productivity, and precision in AI interactions.

Whether you're developing chatbots, writing assistants, virtual tutors, or intelligent search engines, prompt engineering empowers you to shape the model's behavior, tone, and output quality. As AI continues to advance, prompt engineering will play a pivotal role in building responsible, fair, and effective AI systems.

Ready to become a prompt engineering expert? Start experimenting, iterate on your prompts, and keep up with the latest techniques and tools in this dynamic field!

23. Using OpenAI API to Build AI-Powered Apps

Artificial Intelligence (AI) is revolutionizing the way applications work, making them smarter, more interactive, and highly efficient. OpenAI's API provides a powerful and accessible way to integrate AI capabilities into your apps, enabling features like natural language processing (NLP), content generation, chatbot interactions, and more. Whether you're a developer, entrepreneur, or business owner, leveraging the OpenAI API can give your app a competitive edge.

In this article, we'll explore how to use the OpenAI API to build AI-powered applications, covering its capabilities, setup process, and real-world applications.

What is the OpenAI API?

The OpenAI API provides developers access to powerful AI models like GPT-4, which can generate human-like text, answer questions, summarize content, and even assist with coding. The API can be used to build applications that require intelligent text processing, making it ideal for chatbots, customer support, content creation, and more.

Key Capabilities:

- **Natural Language Understanding & Generation** – Process and generate human-like text.
- **Text Summarization** – Convert long-form text into concise summaries.
- **Chatbots & Virtual Assistants** – Develop AI-driven conversational agents.
- **Code Assistance** – Help with debugging, generating, and optimizing code.
- **Language Translation** – Translate text into different languages.

How to Get Started with OpenAI API

Step 1: Sign Up and Get API Key

To use the OpenAI API, you need an API key. Follow these steps:

1. Go to OpenAI's website and sign up.
2. Navigate to the API section and create an account.
3. Obtain your API key from the dashboard.

Step 2: Install OpenAI Python SDK

You can interact with OpenAI's API using various programming languages, but Python is the most commonly used. Install the OpenAI SDK using:

pip install openai

Step 3: Make Your First API Call

Once installed, you can make an API call to generate text. Here's a simple example using Python:

```python
from openai import OpenAI
#we need to export the openAI API key to the environment before using it.
client = OpenAI()

response= client.chat.completions.create(
    model="gpt-4",
    messages=[{"role": "user", "content": "Books of Rajamanickam
Antonimuthu"}],

)
print (response.choices[0].message.content)
```

This script sends a prompt to GPT-4 and prints the response.

Real-World Applications of OpenAI API

1. AI Chatbots and Virtual Assistants

Businesses are using AI-powered chatbots for customer support, FAQs, and virtual assistance. OpenAI's API can handle complex queries, making it an excellent choice for interactive bots.

Example: A customer support chatbot that helps users troubleshoot issues without human intervention.

2. AI-Generated Content

Content creators and marketers can use the OpenAI API to generate blog posts, product descriptions, ad copy, and more.

Example: An e-commerce store using AI to generate product descriptions dynamically.

3. Code Assistance for Developers

Developers can use OpenAI's Codex model (a part of GPT) to generate code snippets, fix errors, and get programming guidance.

Example: A coding assistant that suggests bug fixes or code optimizations in real time.

4. AI-Powered Writing Assistants

Applications like Grammarly and Jasper AI use AI for grammar correction, content suggestions, and improving writing quality.

Example: A blogging platform that suggests edits and enhancements in real time.

5. AI-Based Personalization

AI can analyze user behavior and provide personalized recommendations, improving user engagement.

Example: A news aggregator that tailors articles based on user preferences.

Best Practices for Using OpenAI API

1. **Optimize API Calls** – Avoid unnecessary API calls to minimize costs and response time.
2. **Use Prompt Engineering** – Carefully craft prompts to get the best responses from the model.
3. **Handle API Rate Limits** – Respect OpenAI's rate limits and optimize requests accordingly.
4. **Ensure Data Privacy** – Avoid sharing sensitive information with the API.
5. **Monitor Performance** – Regularly analyze the API's responses to improve accuracy and relevance.

Integrating the OpenAI API into your applications can unlock powerful AI-driven features, making them more intelligent, efficient, and engaging. Whether you're building chatbots, content generators, coding assistants, or personalized apps, OpenAI's API provides a simple yet effective way to implement AI capabilities.

Start experimenting with the OpenAI API today and take your applications to the next level with AI!

24. Building a Simple Retrieval-Augmented Generation (RAG) System with LangChain

Retrieval-Augmented Generation (RAG) is a powerful technique that combines retrieval-based search with a generative AI model. It allows an AI assistant to fetch relevant information from a knowledge base before generating a response, making it more accurate and informative. In this post, we'll walk through building a simple RAG pipeline using LangChain and Hugging Face models.

What is RAG?

RAG improves upon standard AI models by retrieving relevant documents from a database before generating a response. This helps the model provide more contextually accurate answers, especially when dealing with specialized knowledge.

Key Components of a RAG System

1. **Document Storage**: A collection of text documents containing useful information.
2. **Text Splitting**: Divides large documents into smaller, manageable chunks.
3. **Embedding Model**: Converts text chunks into numerical vectors for efficient retrieval.
4. **Vector Database**: Stores embeddings and allows similarity searches.
5. **Retriever**: Fetches the most relevant document chunk for a query.
6. **LLM (Large Language Model)**: Generates answers using the retrieved context.

Step-by-Step Implementation

Step 1: Install Required Libraries

Before we begin, ensure you have the required Python packages installed:

pip install langchain langchain_huggingface faiss-cpu

Step 2: Load and Prepare Documents

We start by defining a set of documents containing useful information:

```
documents = [
    " blah blah blah blah blah blah. blah blah blahblah blah blah. Vitamin C
helps boost immunity.blah blah blah blah blah blah. blah blah blahblah blah
blah.blah blah blah blah blah blah. blah blah blahblah blah blah.",
    "blah blah blah blah blah blah. Exercise improves mental and physical
health. blah blah blah blah blah blah. blah blah.blah blah blah blah blah
blah. blah blah blahblah blah blah.",
    " blah blah blahblah blah blah.blah blah blah blah blah blah. blah blah
blahblah blah blah. Drinking enough water keeps you hydrated and improves
focus. blah blah blah blah blah blah. blah blah blahblah blah blah.blah
blah blah blah blah blah. blah blah blahblah blah blah.blah blah blah blah
blah blah.."
]
```

Since documents are usually long, we need to split them into smaller chunks.

Step 3: Convert Documents into Chunks

```
from langchain.text_splitter import CharacterTextSplitter
text_splitter = CharacterTextSplitter(chunk_size=60, chunk_overlap=10,
separator=".")
chunks = text_splitter.create_documents(documents)
```

This ensures that each chunk is of a manageable size while maintaining some overlap for context.

Step 4: Create Embeddings and Store in Vector Database

We now convert these text chunks into embeddings and store them in FAISS (a fast similarity search database).

```
from langchain_huggingface import HuggingFaceEmbeddings
from langchain_community.vectorstores import FAISS
embeddings =
HuggingFaceEmbeddings(model_name="sentence-transformers/all-MiniLM-L6-v2")
vector_db = FAISS.from_documents(chunks, embeddings)
```

The **Hugging Face embedding model** converts each chunk into a vector representation, making it searchable.

Step 5: Set Up the Chat Model and Retriever

```
from langchain_huggingface import HuggingFaceEndpoint

llm = HuggingFaceEndpoint(repo_id="HuggingFaceH4/zephyr-7b-alpha")
retriever = vector_db.as_retriever(search_kwargs={"k": 1})  # Retrieve only
the most relevant chunk
```

The retriever will find the most relevant document chunk for each query.

Step 6: Define the RAG Chain

We define a prompt template to instruct the LLM on how to use the retrieved context.

```
from langchain.chains import create_retrieval_chain
from langchain.chains.combine_documents import create_stuff_documents_chain
from langchain_core.prompts import PromptTemplate
prompt = PromptTemplate.from_template(
    "You are a helpful AI assistant. Based on the following retrieved
context, answer the question concisely.\n\n"
    "Context:\n{context}\n\n"
    "Question: {input}\n"
    "Answer:"
)
stuff_chain = create_stuff_documents_chain(llm, prompt)
rag_chain = create_retrieval_chain(retriever, stuff_chain)
```

Here, we use **create_stuff_documents_chain** to format the retrieved document before passing it to the LLM.

Step 7: Query and Get a Response

```
query = "How does exercise affect health?"
response = rag_chain.invoke({"input": query})
print("Final Answer:", response["answer"])
```

Now, when you ask a question, the retriever fetches the most relevant document chunk, and the LLM generates an informed answer based on that context.

```
============================================
Final Answer:  Exercise positively impacts both physical and men
es overall body composition. Additionally, regular exercise can
raj@qpt:~/Public/raj/learn$ 
```

Debugging: What is Being Sent to the LLM?

To inspect what is being sent to the LLM, we can print the final prompt:

```python
def debug_rag_chain(input_query):
    retrieved_docs = retriever.get_relevant_documents(input_query)
    retrieved_text = "\n".join([doc.page_content for doc in retrieved_docs])
    formatted_prompt = prompt.format(context=retrieved_text,
input=input_query)
    print("\n===== DEBUG: FINAL PROMPT SENT TO LLM =====\n")
    print(formatted_prompt)
    print("\n=========================================\n")

# Test Debugging
debug_rag_chain("How does exercise affect health?")
```

This helps us understand how the retrieved documents influence the final answer.

By following these steps, we've successfully built a simple **RAG (Retrieval-Augmented Generation) system** using LangChain and Hugging Face. This approach allows us to retrieve relevant information before generating an answer, leading to more accurate and informed responses.

Key Takeaways:

- **RAG improves AI-generated responses by retrieving relevant documents.**
- **We used FAISS as our vector store for efficient document retrieval.**
- **We limited retrieval to the most relevant document chunk for better accuracy.**
- **Debugging helps understand what the LLM is processing**

25. Using Streamlit for AI Development

Artificial Intelligence (AI) is transforming industries, and developers are increasingly looking for ways to deploy AI models with interactive, user-friendly interfaces. **Streamlit** is a powerful Python framework that allows you to quickly build and deploy AI applications with minimal effort. With just a few lines of code, you can create dynamic web applications for showcasing AI models, visualizing data, and providing interactive experiences.

In this chapter, we will explore how Streamlit simplifies AI development and guide you through building an AI-powered app using this framework with free models from **Hugging Face**.

Why Use Streamlit for AI Development?

Streamlit is an open-source Python library designed for simplicity and ease of use. Here's why it is an excellent choice for AI development:

1. **Quick Prototyping** – Build AI demos in minutes using simple Python scripts.
2. **No Frontend Expertise Required** – No need for HTML, CSS, or JavaScript knowledge.
3. **Interactive Widgets** – Add sliders, buttons, text inputs, and file uploads with ease.
4. **Live Model Interaction** – Deploy AI models in a real-time interactive environment.
5. **Easy Deployment** – Deploy apps using Streamlit Cloud, Hugging Face Spaces, or other cloud platforms.

Setting Up Streamlit

To get started, install Streamlit and the Hugging Face Transformers library using pip:

pip install streamlit transformers

You can check if Streamlit is installed correctly by running:

streamlit hello

This command launches a sample Streamlit app to demonstrate its capabilities.

Building a Simple AI-Powered App with Streamlit and Hugging Face

Let's build a **text summarization** app using a free model from Hugging Face.

Step 1: Import Required Libraries

```python
import streamlit as st
from transformers import pipeline

model_name = "sshleifer/distilbart-cnn-12-6"
revision = "a4f8f3e"

# Load Hugging Face summarization model
summarizer = pipeline("summarization", model=model_name, revision=revision)
```

Step 2: Create a Simple UI

Streamlit makes it easy to add UI elements like text inputs, buttons, and sliders.

```python
st.title("AI-Powered Text Summarizer")
st.write("Enter text below and get a concise summary powered by AI.")

user_input = st.text_area("Enter your text:")
```

Step 3: Use the Hugging Face Model to Generate a Summary

```python
if st.button("Summarize"):
    if user_input:
        summary = summarizer(user_input, max_length=100, min_length=30,
do_sample=False)
        st.subheader("Summary:")
        st.write(summary[0]["summary_text"])
    else:
        st.warning("Please enter text to summarize.")
```

Step 4: Run the App

Save the script as app.py and run the following command:

streamlit run app.py

This will launch a web app where users can enter text and receive AI-generated summaries.

Deploying the Streamlit App

Once your app is ready, you can deploy it on **Streamlit Cloud** or **Hugging Face Spaces**.

Deploying on Hugging Face Spaces:

1. Create an account on Hugging Face.
2. Go to **Spaces** and create a new space.
3. Select **Streamlit** as the app type.
4. Push your app's files to the repository.
5. Your app will be hosted for free on Hugging Face!

Streamlit is a game-changer for AI developers, allowing them to build interactive AI applications quickly and efficiently. With its user-friendly interface and seamless integration with Hugging Face models, Streamlit makes AI deployment more accessible than ever.

Start experimenting with Streamlit today and bring your AI models to life with engaging web applications!

26. Creating a Local Chatbot Using Popular AI Models

Chatbots have become an essential tool for businesses and developers, enabling automated interactions and improving user engagement. While cloud-based APIs like OpenAI and Google Bard are popular, many developers prefer running chatbots locally for **better control, privacy, and cost savings**. Thanks to open-source AI models, creating a **fully local chatbot** is easier than ever.

In this guide, we'll walk you through setting up a local chatbot using **LLama 2, Mistral, Vicuna, and Rasa**, some of the most actively used open-source AI models.

Why Build a Local Chatbot?

Running a chatbot locally has several advantages:

1. **Privacy & Security** – Keep conversations confidential without relying on external servers.
2. **Cost Efficiency** – Avoid API costs and subscription fees.
3. **Offline Access** – No dependency on internet connectivity for chatbot interactions.
4. **Customization** – Fine-tune the model for your specific needs.

Choosing the Right Model

Several open-source AI models can power a local chatbot. Here are four of the most actively used:

1. **Llama 2 (by Meta)** – A powerful, efficient model available in 7B, 13B, and 65B parameter versions. Ideal for general conversations.
2. **Mistral** – A lightweight, high-performance model known for speed and efficiency.
3. **Vicuna** – Fine-tuned for conversational AI, providing high-quality chatbot-like responses.
4. **Rasa** – An intent-based chatbot framework that allows for structured dialogue and advanced conversation handling.

All of these models can be run locally using **Ollama, GPTQ, Llama.cpp, or Rasa's framework**.

Setting Up a Local Chatbot

Step 1: Install Required Dependencies

To run a chatbot locally, you'll need a framework to load and interact with the model. Popular choices include:

- **Ollama** (Easiest setup for Llama 2 and Mistral)

- **Llama.cpp** (Lightweight and optimized for CPU/GPU usage)
- **Text Generation WebUI** (User-friendly web interface for multiple models)
- **Rasa** (Best for intent-based chatbots with structured conversations)

Install Ollama (Recommended for Beginners)

curl -fsSL https://ollama.com/install.sh | sh

Install Llama.cpp (For Advanced Users)

git clone https://github.com/ggerganov/llama.cpp.git

cd llama.cpp

make

Install Rasa (For Intent-Based Chatbots)

pip install rasa

Step 2: Download the Model

Once the environment is ready, download a chatbot model.

Using Ollama to Download Llama 2

ollama pull meta/llama2

Using Hugging Face for Mistral or Vicuna

git clone https://huggingface.co/TheBloke/Mistral-7B-GGUF

Initializing a Rasa Project

rasa init

This command sets up the basic directory structure and example chatbot.

Step 3: Running the Chatbot

Once the model is downloaded, you can start the chatbot.

Start a Chatbot with Ollama

ollama run llama2

Start a Chatbot with Llama.cpp

./main -m models/llama2.gguf -p "Hello, how can I help you?"

Start a Chatbot with Rasa

rasa train

rasa shell

This will launch an interactive chatbot where you can test intent-based conversations.

Step 4: Creating a Simple Python Interface

To create a user-friendly chatbot, use Python and Streamlit.

```python
import streamlit as st
import subprocess

def query_model(prompt):
    result = subprocess.run(["ollama", "run", "llama2", prompt],
capture_output=True, text=True)
    return result.stdout

st.title("Local AI Chatbot")
prompt = st.text_input("Ask me anything:")
if st.button("Send"):
    response = query_model(prompt)
```

```
st.write(response)
```

Run the script:

streamlit run chatbot.py

This will launch a local web interface where users can chat with the model.

Building a local chatbot is now easier than ever with powerful open-source AI models. Whether you use **Llama 2, Mistral, Vicuna, or Rasa**, these models provide **high-quality conversational AI** while ensuring **privacy, cost savings, and full control**.

- If you need a **fully conversational AI chatbot**, use Llama 2, Mistral, or Vicuna.
- If you want a chatbot with **structured intent recognition and dialogue management**, Rasa is the best choice.

Start experimenting today and deploy your **own AI chatbot locally!**

27. DeepSeek AI Development: A New Era of Open-Source AI

DeepSeek AI is an emerging open-source AI framework designed to push the boundaries of **natural language processing (NLP), machine learning (ML), and deep learning**. With a strong focus on **efficiency, scalability, and accessibility**, DeepSeek AI provides developers with state-of-the-art models that can be deployed across various applications, from chatbots to document summarization and beyond.

In this chapter, we'll explore **DeepSeek AI's capabilities, how to set up a development environment, and how to create AI-powered applications** using its models.

Why DeepSeek AI?

DeepSeek AI stands out for several reasons:

1. **Open-Source & Transparent** – Unlike proprietary models, DeepSeek AI offers full access to its code, making it customizable.
2. **Optimized for Efficiency** – Designed for both **CPU and GPU** deployment, enabling smoother local and cloud-based execution.
3. **Pre-trained & Fine-Tunable** – Comes with robust **pre-trained models** while allowing for domain-specific fine-tuning.
4. **Multi-Language Support** – Expands NLP capabilities beyond English to multiple languages.
5. **Scalability** – Supports enterprise and research-grade AI solutions.

Setting Up DeepSeek AI for Development

Before you can start developing with DeepSeek AI, you need to set up the right environment.

Step 1: Install Dependencies

DeepSeek AI requires **Python 3.8+** and essential ML libraries. Start by setting up a virtual environment:

```
python -m venv deepseek_env

source deepseek_env/bin/activate  # On Windows: deepseek_env\Scripts\activate
```

Then, install the necessary packages:

```
pip install torch transformers deepseek
```

If using a **GPU**, install the CUDA-optimized PyTorch:

```
pip install torch torchvision torchaudio --index-url https://download.pytorch.org/whl/cu118
```

Running a Pre-Trained DeepSeek Model

DeepSeek provides **powerful pre-trained LLMs (Large Language Models)** that can be used for NLP tasks.

Example: Using DeepSeek for Text Generation

```
from transformers import AutoModelForCausalLM, AutoTokenizer

# Load the DeepSeek model
tokenizer = AutoTokenizer.from_pretrained("deepseek-ai/deepseek-llm")
model = AutoModelForCausalLM.from_pretrained("deepseek-ai/deepseek-llm")

# Generate a response
input_text = "What are the benefits of AI in healthcare?"
input_ids = tokenizer.encode(input_text, return_tensors="pt")
output = model.generate(input_ids, max_length=100)
response = tokenizer.decode(output[0], skip_special_tokens=True)

print(response)
```

Fine-Tuning DeepSeek AI

If you need a **custom chatbot, document summarizer, or domain-specific AI**, you can fine-tune DeepSeek AI with your dataset.

Step 1: Prepare Your Dataset

Your dataset should be in JSON format, like this:

```
{
  "text": "Artificial Intelligence is transforming the world by automating tasks and providing insights."
}
```

Step 2: Fine-Tune the Model

Using Hugging Face's `Trainer` API, you can fine-tune DeepSeek AI:

```
from transformers import Trainer, TrainingArguments

def train_model():
    training_args = TrainingArguments(
        output_dir="./deepseek-finetuned",
        evaluation_strategy="epoch",
```

```
        per_device_train_batch_size=8,
        per_device_eval_batch_size=8,
        num_train_epochs=3,
        save_steps=10_000,
        save_total_limit=2,
    )
    trainer = Trainer(
        model=model,
        args=training_args,
        train_dataset=your_train_dataset,
        eval_dataset=your_eval_dataset
    )
    trainer.train()

train_model()
```

Deploying DeepSeek AI

Once your model is trained, you can deploy it using **FastAPI** or **Streamlit** for real-world applications.

Example: Deploying a Chatbot with Streamlit

```
import streamlit as st

def chat_with_ai(prompt):
    input_ids = tokenizer.encode(prompt, return_tensors="pt")
    output = model.generate(input_ids, max_length=100)
    return tokenizer.decode(output[0], skip_special_tokens=True)

st.title("DeepSeek AI Chatbot")
user_input = st.text_input("Ask me anything:")
if st.button("Send"):
    response = chat_with_ai(user_input)
    st.write(response)
```

Run the script:

streamlit run chatbot.py

This will launch a local chatbot using DeepSeek AI.

DeepSeek AI is a **powerful, open-source AI framework** that offers flexibility for AI developers. Whether you need a **pre-trained model** for instant use, fine-tuning capabilities for custom applications, or **deployment options for real-world AI**, DeepSeek AI is an excellent choice.

28. Exploring Neural Networks with TensorFlow Playground

Artificial Intelligence (AI) and Machine Learning (ML) can seem complex, especially when it comes to neural networks. However, **TensorFlow Playground** provides an interactive way to visualize and experiment with neural networks right from your browser—no coding required! In this chapter, we'll explore what TensorFlow Playground is, how it works, and how you can use it to understand deep learning concepts.

What is TensorFlow Playground?

TensorFlow Playground is a web-based tool that allows users to experiment with **neural networks** in an interactive way. It provides a visual interface to tweak **neurons, layers, activation functions, and training parameters** while immediately seeing the effect on model performance.

🔗 You can access TensorFlow Playground here: https://playground.tensorflow.org

Why Use TensorFlow Playground?

- **No Coding Required** – Explore deep learning concepts visually.
- **Interactive Learning** – Adjust parameters and see real-time changes.
- **Great for Beginners** – Understand how neural networks learn from data.
- **Quick Experimentation** – Test different architectures in seconds.

Key Features and How They Work

1. The Dataset Selection

At the top-left, you'll find a section where you can choose a dataset. TensorFlow Playground provides different datasets, including:

✔ **Linear classification** – Simple data with two separable classes.

✔ **Non-linear classification** – More complex patterns that require deeper networks.

👉 **Tip:** Start with a simple dataset and gradually increase complexity to see how the model adapts.

---

2. Neural Network Architecture

On the right, you can customize your **neural network structure**:

- **Input Layer** – Features (x1, x2) that the model uses.
- **Hidden Layers** – Intermediate layers where the network learns patterns.
- **Output Layer** – Produces the final classification or regression result.

👉 **Tip:** Adding more **hidden layers** can help with complex patterns, but too many layers can lead to overfitting.

---

3. Activation Functions

Activation functions determine how neurons pass information. TensorFlow Playground allows you to choose from:

- **ReLU (Rectified Linear Unit)** – Good for deep networks.
- **Sigmoid** – Useful for probabilities but prone to vanishing gradients.
- **Tanh** – Works well but can still suffer from vanishing gradients.
- **Linear** – Used in regression tasks.

👉 **Tip: ReLU** is commonly used for hidden layers, while **sigmoid** or **softmax** is used for the output layer.

---

4. Training Controls

- **Learning Rate** – Controls how quickly the model updates weights.
- **Epochs (Steps)** – Number of times the model sees the data.
- **Regularization (L1/L2)** – Prevents overfitting by penalizing large weights.
- **Batch Size** – How many samples are used per training step.

☛ **Tip:** If your model learns too slowly, increase the **learning rate** slightly, but not too much, or it might not converge.

Hands-on Experiment: Building a Simple Neural Network

1. Choose the **"Circle" dataset** (a non-linear dataset).
2. Set **two hidden layers** with **4 and 3 neurons** each.
3. Use **ReLU** as the activation function.
4. Set the **learning rate** to 0.01.
5. Click **Run** and observe how the network learns over time!

■ **What to observe?** Watch how the decision boundary (the colored area) evolves as the network trains. If it's too simple, try adding more layers or neurons.

Pros and Cons of TensorFlow Playground

■ Pros:

✔ **Easy to use** – No setup required.

✔ **Great for beginners** – Visualizes neural network training.

✔ **Quick experiments** – Test different architectures instantly.

✗ Cons:

✘ **Limited datasets** – Only small 2D datasets are available.

✘ **Not for real-world training** – Cannot train large-scale models.

✘ **Basic features only** – Lacks advanced ML techniques like CNNs and RNNs.

How to Improve Further?

- **Experiment with deeper networks** – See how additional layers affect learning.
- **Play with regularization** – Try **L1/L2 regularization** to prevent overfitting.
- **Change learning rates** – Observe how different learning rates impact model convergence.
- **Compare activation functions** – Test different functions and compare their effects.

TensorFlow Playground is a fantastic tool for **learning neural networks visually**. Whether you're new to AI or just want to experiment with different architectures, it offers an easy way to **grasp deep learning fundamentals** without writing a single line of code.

So go ahead—**play around, experiment, and learn!**

29. AI Development Best Practices

Artificial Intelligence (AI) development is revolutionizing industries by enabling automation, enhancing decision-making, and creating intelligent applications. However, building and deploying AI models require careful planning and adherence to best practices to ensure efficiency, fairness, and scalability.

In this guide, we will cover essential AI development best practices, including **data preparation, model selection, ethical considerations, deployment strategies, and performance monitoring**.

---

1. Understanding Business Goals and Problem Definition

Before starting AI development, it is crucial to define the **business goals** and **problem statement** clearly:

- Identify **what problem AI is solving** (e.g., fraud detection, chatbot, recommendation system).
- Ensure AI is **the right tool** for the problem; sometimes rule-based automation may suffice.
- Define clear **KPIs (Key Performance Indicators)** to measure success.

---

2. Data Collection and Preparation

2.1. Data Quality Matters

Data is the backbone of AI models. Follow these principles:

- **Ensure high-quality data** by removing duplicates, errors, and inconsistencies.
- **Collect diverse datasets** to avoid biases and ensure generalizability.
- **Balance datasets** to prevent class imbalance in classification tasks.

2.2. Data Preprocessing

Data must be cleaned and formatted before training:

- **Tokenization & Normalization** for NLP models.
- **Feature scaling & normalization** for numerical datasets.
- **Data augmentation** for image-based AI.
- **Handling missing values** using imputation techniques.

2.3. Data Privacy & Security

- Follow **GDPR and CCPA** regulations for handling user data.
- Implement **data anonymization** when necessary.
- Use **secure storage and encryption** to protect sensitive information.

---

3. Choosing the Right AI Model

3.1. Selecting the Model Architecture

The choice of AI model depends on the problem type:

- **Supervised Learning**: Classification and regression tasks (e.g., Decision Trees, Random Forest, Neural Networks).
- **Unsupervised Learning**: Clustering and pattern detection (e.g., K-Means, Autoencoders).
- **Reinforcement Learning**: Decision-making agents (e.g., Q-learning, PPO).

3.2. Pretrained vs. Custom Models

- **Pretrained Models** (e.g., BERT, GPT, ResNet) are useful for transfer learning and reducing training time.
- **Custom Models** are required when domain-specific tuning is needed.

---

4. Model Training and Optimization

4.1. Avoid Overfitting

- Use **dropout layers, regularization (L1/L2)**, and **early stopping**.
- Increase **dataset size** or use augmentation techniques.

4.2. Hyperparameter Tuning

- Optimize parameters using **Grid Search, Random Search, or Bayesian Optimization**.
- Fine-tune **learning rates, batch sizes, and network architectures**.

4.3. Training Efficiency

- Utilize **GPU acceleration (e.g., NVIDIA CUDA, TensorFlow, PyTorch)**.
- Apply **distributed training** for large-scale datasets.

---

5. Model Evaluation and Validation

5.1. Performance Metrics

Evaluate models using appropriate metrics:

- **Classification:** Accuracy, Precision, Recall, F1-score, ROC-AUC.
- **Regression:** Mean Squared Error (MSE), R-squared.
- **NLP:** BLEU, ROUGE, perplexity.

5.2. Cross-Validation

- Use **k-fold cross-validation** to ensure robustness.
- Avoid **data leakage** by properly splitting train, validation, and test sets.

---

6. Ethical AI and Bias Mitigation

6.1. Identifying and Reducing Bias

- Perform **Fairness Audits** to detect biases in datasets and models.
- Use **explainable AI (XAI)** techniques to understand decision-making.
- Incorporate **diverse datasets** to prevent discriminatory outcomes.

6.2. Transparent and Responsible AI

- Follow AI **ethics guidelines** from organizations like IEEE and EU AI Act.
- Maintain **accountability** by logging AI decisions and keeping audit trails.

---

7. Model Deployment Best Practices

7.1. Choosing the Right Deployment Strategy

- **Cloud-based (AWS, GCP, Azure)**: Scalable but may have latency.
- **Edge AI (on-device models)**: Best for real-time processing.
- **Hybrid (cloud + edge)**: Balances performance and cost.

7.2. Containerization & API Integration

- Use **Docker & Kubernetes** for scalable AI deployment.
- Deploy AI models as **RESTful APIs** with Flask or FastAPI.

```python
from fastapi import FastAPI
import torch
from transformers import AutoModelForCausalLM, AutoTokenizer

app = FastAPI()
model = AutoModelForCausalLM.from_pretrained("gpt2")
tokenizer = AutoTokenizer.from_pretrained("gpt2")

@app.post("/predict")
def predict(text: str):
    input_ids = tokenizer.encode(text, return_tensors="pt")
    output = model.generate(input_ids, max_length=100)
    return {"response": tokenizer.decode(output[0],
skip_special_tokens=True)}
```

---

8. Monitoring and Maintenance

8.1. Continuous Monitoring

- Set up **model drift detection** to check for performance degradation.
- Use tools like **Prometheus, Grafana, or MLflow** for monitoring.

8.2. Regular Model Updates

- Periodically retrain models with fresh data.
- Apply **A/B testing** before rolling out updates.

AI development is an evolving field, and following best practices ensures reliable, ethical, and scalable AI solutions. **By focusing on data quality, model robustness, ethical AI, and efficient deployment, you can build AI systems that deliver real-world impact.**

Start implementing these best practices today and elevate your AI development journey!

30. Conclusion and Next Steps

Congratulations! You've taken your first steps into the fascinating world of Artificial Intelligence. From understanding the basics of AI to exploring its applications, ethical implications, and future potential, you've gained a solid foundation to build upon. In this final chapter, we'll recap the key takeaways from this ebook and guide you on how to continue your AI journey.

Key Takeaways

Let's revisit some of the most important lessons from this ebook:
1. **AI is Everywhere:** From smartphones to healthcare, AI is already transforming our lives in countless ways.
2. **Machine Learning is the Heart of AI:** It's the technology that enables AI systems to learn from data and improve over time.
3. **Data is the Fuel:** High-quality data is essential for building effective AI systems.
4. **Ethics Matter:** As AI advances, it's crucial to address issues like bias, privacy, and accountability.
5. **The Future is Bright:** AI has the potential to solve some of humanity's biggest challenges, but it also comes with responsibilities.

How to Continue Your AI Journey

Your journey into AI doesn't end here. Here are some actionable steps to keep learning and growing:

---

1. Keep Learning
- **Online Courses**: There are numerous online platforms offering beginner-to-advanced AI courses, covering everything from fundamental concepts to cutting-edge research.
- **Books**: Explore well-regarded books on artificial intelligence, machine learning, and deep learning to deepen your theoretical understanding and practical knowledge.
- **Video Tutorials**: Follow educational video content to stay updated on the latest trends, breakthroughs, and practical applications in AI

To continuously improve your AI skills, make it a habit to check these essential resources daily:

- **AI News & Research:** Follow platforms like ArXiv.org and Papers with Code for the latest AI research papers and breakthroughs.
- **Industry Blogs & Newsletters:** Subscribe to DeepLearning.AI, and Import AI for expert insights.
- **Hands-on Learning:** Regularly explore AI tools on Hugging Face and experiment with open-source models on GitHub.

By consistently learning and staying engaged with the AI community, you'll stay ahead of the curve and continue growing as an AI expert.

---

2. Practice, Practice, Practice

- **Work on Projects:** Apply what you've learned by working on small AI projects. Start with the fun projects we discussed in Chapter 11.
- **Join Competitions:** Participate in online challenges on platforms like Kaggle to test your skills and learn from others.

---

3. Build a Portfolio

- Showcase your skills by creating a portfolio of AI projects. This could include anything from a simple chatbot to a machine learning model that predicts housing prices.
- Share your work on platforms like GitHub or LinkedIn to attract potential employers or collaborators.

---

4. Join the AI Community

- **Online Forums:** Engage with AI enthusiasts on platforms like Reddit (e.g., r/MachineLearning) or Stack Overflow.
- **Meetups and Conferences:** Attend AI meetups, webinars, or conferences to network and learn from experts.
- **Social Media:** Follow AI thought leaders and organizations on Twitter, LinkedIn, and other platforms.

---

5. Stay Curious and Open-Minded

- AI is a rapidly evolving field, so stay curious and keep exploring new ideas and technologies.
- Don't be afraid to ask questions, experiment, and make mistakes—it's all part of the learning process.

Final Thoughts

Artificial Intelligence is one of the most exciting and transformative technologies of our time. Whether you're interested in pursuing a career in AI, using it to solve real-world problems, or simply understanding how it works, the possibilities are endless. Remember, the journey of learning AI is just as important as the destination. Stay curious, keep experimenting, and most importantly, have fun!

Thank You for Reading!

I hope this book has inspired you to explore the world of AI and given you the tools to get started. The future of AI is in your hands—what will you create?

You can send your feedback and suggestions to rajamanickam.a@gmail.com Contact me if you need one-on-one coaching to learn AI, especially RAG or Snowflakes/SQL.

Check below my other ebooks.

- Mastering SQL: A Comprehensive Guide to Database Mastery
- Retrieval-Augmented Generation (RAG): The Future of AI-Powered Knowledge Retrieval
- Dream Big, Move Forward Inch by Inch: A Simple and Effective Guide for Finding Happiness and Success in Your Life
- AI Insights into the Bible
- Mastering Snowflake: A Beginner's Guide to Cloud Data Warehousing

www.ingramcontent.com/pod-product-compliance
Lightning Source LLC
LaVergne TN
LVHW081758050326
832903LV00027B/2005